Caring for the Caregivers

CARING
for the
CAREGIVERS

C. W. BRISTER

BROADMAN PRESS
Nashville, Tennessee

© Copyright 1985 • Broadman Press
All rights reserved
4255-37
ISBN: 0-8054-5537-X

Dewey Decimal Classification: 253.2
Subject Headings: MINISTERS // MISSIONARIES
Library of Congress Catalog Card Number: 85-3793
Printed in the United States of America

Library of Congress Cataloging in Publication Data

Brister, C. W.
    Caring for the caregivers.

    Includes index.
    1. Southern Baptist Convention—Clergy—Religious
life.   2. Missionaries—Religious life.   3. Southern
Baptist Convention—Clergy—Psychology.   4. Missionaries—
Psychology.   I. Title.
BX6345.B75   1985   253'.2   85-3793
ISBN 0-8054-5537-X

To our students and the staff

Baptist Seminary of East Africa

Limuru, Kenya
Branch

In fond remembrance and profound hope

Contents

Foreword

Truman S. Smith

Senior Family Consultant, Foreign Mission Board,
Southern Baptist Convention

Reading this manuscript has been a personal adventure for me. I know some of the persons whose experiences come alive in these pages. Most of the others' stories reflect and clarify the human scene that I experience as a caregiver.

More than this, I have been led through my own history with fresh understanding of resources received, including special care from friends and some strangers along the way. This book served as a reminder of my debt to scores of caring persons and as a prompter of my supportive interest for my own pastor and church staff.

Expectations to succeed touch our lives in persistent, blatant fashion. There are many marketplace reminders of the need to dress for success, fail-safe ways to close a sale, and methods of moving to the top in one's organization or profession. These messages touch all ages. Even children are encouraged to ask for a particular kind of toy, doll, or clothes to assure that they will be approved by their friends.

To fall short of personal and professional ideals in ministry, whether as professional ministers in the United States or as missionaries overseas, means high risk from two sources. First, one might fail in the perfecting of ideals in his or her walk with God, and, second, one may not live up to the complex expectations of persons to whom ministry is extended. The message of hope and salvation, intended as good news, may be contaminated by such internal and external pressures.

9

In the seasons of my life, there have been times for soul-searching during lonely vigils while at other times I have laughed, loved, and celebrated in a lively community of faith. I have not always been receptive to care offered by other persons, nor faithful to extend care to folks near at hand. The human need to maintain separateness and pretense of self-sufficiency is enough to hold at arm's length even the most energetic comforter. This volume is a timely reminder that the windows and doors of our spirits may be nudged open a bit, from without or within, unless secured locks keep persons from sharing our pain.

Dr. Brister shares lively resources for those who will use them, leading to the removal of bolted locks from life's doors and windows so that passages may be opened between caregivers and those who would provide care for them. Empathy in its way is therapy. Understanding helps to alleviate suffering.

On one occasion, I was present at the closing session of an orientation program for new missionaries. They had been together for eight weeks as individuals, couples, and families. Their common commitment and rigorous schedules had encouraged a strong sense of community and identification with one another. On departure day feelings ran deep in the group. One person remarked, with choked voice and blotting of tears, that they all seemed allergic to saying good-bye. These persons reflected great variety of history, training, and experience. Each individual was dealing with the loss of a meaningful support community in his or her own way—a loss symbolic of all other losses. Most of them acknowledged their developmental limits and needs as they anticipated impossible tasks in various overseas mission assignments. Others conveyed self-assurance, communicating boldness and confidence in their new assignments. In hearing the stories of a number of persons, I know how much they were needing the understanding, kindness, support, nurture, acceptance, love, and grace offered by a caregiver who represented more than himself in a larger community of faith.

One of the missionaries had injured an ankle in a basketball game and was on crutches for a while. Back muscles, unaccustomed to the strains of vigorous exercise, cried for help following an injury and trip to the emergency room of a local hospital. Another missionary appointee experienced persistent knee pains which eventually required surgery to remove some bone chips. They formed a fellowship of the handicapped. Each man left walking straight and tall. They had been well cared for because of their obvious needs. My hunch is there were other group members whose private needs were greater, yet who had difficulty sharing those needs with persons at hand. Hence, they were not cared for by the caregivers available to them.

During personal crises of illness and death, support usually comes from members of one's family, friends, and acquaintances. The more difficult times may well be those "lonely nights of the soul" that are not easily acknowledged nor clearly seen by persons close at hand.

The chapters of this book identify the foundations of our faith and the relationships within which resources take shape and form. The realities and possibilities encourage us in order that we might minister to our ministers and care for our caregivers in specific, planned and spontaneous, fashion.

I identify myself as a blessed caregiver. I have waited with loved ones for death to bring release. I have kept vigil with persons who have been crushed in heart and spirit by crisis and have sensed feelings of helplessness as marriage ties have been broken through indifference and carelessness. I have celebrated with others in marriage, birth of children, in job success, wedding anniversary celebrations, even retirement. In each of these relationships, something has gone out of me that needed replacing. Resources were shared, yet not always replenished.

Attention has been divided, with personal and family needs at times poorly met.

I acknowledge with gratitude those individuals who have offered themselves in nurture and support, more often than not unasked, through the years of my ministry. Numbered among these have been Gloria and C. W. Brister. They reflect such differing gifts, yet each complements the other as they provide personal and professional resources for those whose lives mingle with theirs.

Dr. Brister writes from the perspective of the marketplace where people are met as they live their lives. He has found them in the tattered garments of ordinary people with insolvable problems. Caregivers have come to him out of desperation and divisiveness of spirit, out of threats to life and sanity, out of failure and grief, as well as with gladness, joy, and gratitude. They have come as Christian ministers, missionaries, and devoted laypersons. He has supported their ministries from pulpit and pew, from classroom and office, from living room to the byways of Texas, and communities large and small in Africa, Asia, and Latin America. Out of his deep personal commitment to the healing and enabling of ministers and missionaries, this book has grown as a reflection of what his life has been about. It is an outgrowth of meeting personal challenges with strong faith and confident hope in the living Lord.

In his final chapter, the writer reminds us that faith, hope, and love are relational virtues, anchoring us to God and members of the household of faith. I thank God for individuals who have somehow known such relationships through their communion with the Holy Spirit and for others who are yet open to learning the grace of caring for caregivers. Our Lord affirmed the sensitivity and fidelity to the care of such persons thus: "Blessed are the poor in spirit: for theirs is the kingdom of heaven" (Matt. 5:3, KJV).

Preface

Concern for persons who invest their whole lives in Christian mission and ministry is as old as the church itself. In an early letter affirming his own apostleship, Paul wrote: "The Lord commanded that those who proclaim the gospel should get their living by the gospel" (1 Cor. 9:14). Our understanding of Christian proclamation has broadened so that functions of ministers today are diverse and global. According to reliable estimates, more than half a million Americans "proclaim the gospel" vocationally in some ministry occupation. Given their marriages and family ties, a sizable segment of the US population is invested, either directly or indirectly, in church-related employment. Caring for these caregivers is a major ' ~ requiring collaboration of many persons.

The Bible recognizes the common heritage of all believ God's servants, wherever their gifts may be employed in daily vocation. Christ's ministry was interlinked with His disciples' work—like a great vine with many branches (John 15:1-17). Ideally, each church member is a minister, and all believers are kinspersons in God's family. "None of us lives to himself, and none of us dies to himself," regardless of diverse theological positions, denominational labels, and personal life-styles (Rom. 14:7).

Cultures around the world tend, however, to practice a *ministry mystique* of magical attitudes and beliefs concerning religious professionals' lives. While cast together in God's mission on earth, laypersons are tempted to view their spiritual guides through esoteric lenses. Religious leaders throughout history, who have fostered a split-level theology of clergy/laity separation, are largely responsible for what has happened to their relationships. This book attempts a mid-course correction of such separatist views by picturing the human needs of persons in ministry vocations.

Here, I am making available to concerned Christians certain aspects of religious professionals' lives which they might otherwise dismiss at great cost. My goal is to strengthen their connectedness in the mission of God's kingdom on earth. Basically, this is a layperson's book to aid their understanding of servant-leaders who work as ministers and missionaries around the world. The emphasis is positive—sharing and supporting Christ's cause and His workers wherever they may serve.

Having been a pastor, theological educator, volunteer missionary, and international lecturer over a span of thirty-five years, I have lived among and loved the people of whom I write. Christian ministers are my kinsmen, brothers and sisters in the family of faith. For some years, my wife and I served in family enrichment and MK testing at a center where missionaries were oriented before going abroad. Research into the human problems of ministers and their families has been a continuing interest. Also, I have served as a consultant at the associational, state, and national level of our denomination concerning needs ministers face. This book is an attempt to get certain discoveries, observations, and suggestions out into the open.

Have you ever wondered who *ministers* to Christian ministers and missionaries? You may be more involved in the answer than you have previously thought. To look beyond the veil of privacy into the ordinariness, struggles, and aspirations of lives devoted to religious vocations is a rare privilege. Already, you have sensed that the connection between the "real" world and shrouded cloister is only a thin membrane. Professional care-givers are more human than otherwise!

This volume suggests how you can reinforce your minister's sense of calling and identity, enhance his or her self-esteem, nourish Christian vision, foster feelings of emotional security, assist in periods of distress or crisis, help prevent or resolve interpersonal conflicts, strengthen family ties, and thus under-gird God's work. It pictures a support network for caregivers, through shared ministry, that ties believers together as equals in Christ. Both men and women, singles and marrieds, are envisioned by the terms *ministers* and *missionaries.* They each must deal with a sense of divine calling, seek professional education, establish credibility in the ecclesiastical arena, and function through God's assignment. Such religious vocations take them literally to the ends of the earth.

What does it mean to be a minister or missionary in today's world? What is required of men and women who attempt to bring light into the dark places of earth, "good news to the poor, . . . release for prisoners . . . sight for the blind," and practical evidence of God's favor (Luke 4:18-19, NEB)? The pressures on today's ministers are enormous and satisfactions are mixed. No amount of human kindness or care can replace the true servant's hunger for God. He alone supplies spiritual vitality for life. Human friends, however, offer companionship on the journey of faith.

A major purpose of this book is to picture the price of being human in religious vocations. Further, I hope to persuade Christian leaders to allocate resources for enriching the lives of ministry professionals. In addition to current programs, church resources can support activities that accomplish goals like: (1) fostering healthy spirituality, emotional stability, financial security, and companionship covenants of ministry for family members and friends; (2) achieving work objectives with full accountability to God and employer groups; (3) enhancing the quality of life in environments where ministers and missionaries live and work; (4) assisting religious caregivers to achieve their full potential for ministry through a viable support network; and (5) enabling ministers to experience and express the joys of Christian living they offer to others.

In order to ensure privacy and avoid any breach of confidence, all accounts relating to persons in this work (except those quoted from specific authors or for which special permission has been obtained) are either hypothetical or composites based on typical situations. The truths are accurate, but the specific words and people portrayed are dramas of life.

Finally, I express a debt to many people: to the administration and trustees of Southwestern Baptist Theological Seminary for granting a year's sabbatical leave from classroom and committee tasks; to Truman S. Smith, Senior Family Consultant, Foreign Mission Board of the Southern Baptist Convention, for sustaining colleagueship and preparing the Foreword; to missionaries Vance and Cherry Kirkpatrick and Sam and Bonnie Turner, with whom we served in Kenya; and Marion G. (Bud) and Jane Fray and Jewel and Jeanne Franks, with whom we worked in South Africa; to my partners in ministry dialogue—Clyde N. Austin, James L. Cooper, and J. David Fite—and pastor son, Mark A. Brister; researchers Robert Phillips and Steve M. Lyon; typist Dawn Collins; and to Gloria, my life companion and partner in ministry, for her intuitive wisdom, enthusiasm for life, loyal friendship, and unfailing love. She has been an insightful consultant, faithful encourager, and harbinger of peace during this time of strenuous work. And I am grateful to God for health and strength to bring this project to conclusion.

C. W. BRISTER

1 Calling:
"Fools for Christ's Sake"

"I'm forty-nine and facing a major career decision." Jim Cole's voice reached me a thousand miles away by telephone. "I'm afraid to make the wrong move. What do you think of someone my age going into hospital chaplaincy? Would I be leaving the mainstream of ministry?"

Understanding how a person becomes a Christian minister or missionary stretches the limits of a layperson's imagination. The devoted church member lacks precise criteria for verifying factors that point persons into religious vocations. For that matter, some vocational religious workers may be unclear themselves about why they are in the ministry. Yet, the layperson relates to ministers in good faith, trusts that their motives are valid, and opens himself to their authentic pastoral care.

Given the overwhelming diversity of Christian denominational groups in today's world with extremes of doctrine and practice, religious leaders seem a breed apart. They are not exactly laypersons anymore (though they once were), nor do laity wish them to be mere mortals. Some ministers wear clerical collars; others appear in business clothing. Some religious professionals sound so spiritual; others seem rather worldly. Some are scholarly, devout, and well organized; others reflect serious deficits of education, spirituality, and managerial ability. One minister may be a good person but negative or passive —almost good for nothing. Another appears dictatorial, bull-

17

dozing his way through church building programs, budget promotions, and Sunday worship services.

One can ill afford to stereotype ministers as being "all alike." A television preacher promises listeners health, worldly success, and good fortune in return for following his brand of religion. A Catholic priest may live in near poverty as a family brother in some out-of-the-way abbey. Here is a punster, there a comedian; here the prankster, and there a wise, earnest shepherd of souls. One missionary is laid back, casual, and easygoing; another seems visionary, almost driven, in his haste to cross new frontiers of service.

Where can the concerned layperson turn for guidance in understanding personality characteristics of Christian ministers and missionaries? Particularly, what are preferred means of getting to know vocational religious workers and of reaching out to affirm them on their challenging journeys of faith? Perhaps the place to begin is with vignettes from lives of folks who would consider themselves ordinary people in extraordinary callings.

A Look at People on Mission

Most of the ministers and missionaries I know have obeyed a divine summons to share Jesus Christ personally through a life of mission. While such sharing expresses itself in diverse acts of ministry, their prevailing spirit is sincere obedience, spiritual concern, and enthusiasm for God. Assurance of divine appointment helps them cope with many disappointments along life's way. For such reasons, the apostle Paul is one of their favorite biblical guides.

As a missionary pastor, the time came when Paul was forced to defend his ordination from above with the Corinthian congregation which was divided by party strife. "This is how one should regard us, as servants of Christ and stewards of the mysteries of God" (1 Cor. 4:1). Some members of that first-century church were guilty of sexual sins like incest and immorality (1 Cor. 5:1-2; 6:15-17). Others were taking grievances against their Christian brothers into pagan courts (1 Cor. 6:1-6). There were problems in marriage, behavioral indiscretions in worship, inappropriate speaking in tongues, and pride in spiritual gifts (1 Cor. 7; 8:9-11; 11:18-22; 12:1 to 14:5). Party strife had divided the congregation into factions.

In vindicating his apostleship with immature believers and in calling them to loving union with Christ, Paul used a daring metaphor. "I think that God has exhibited us apostles . . . like men sentenced to death; because we have become a spectacle to the world." He was like a criminal on death row, but more! "We are fools for Christ's sake," he chided readers, "but you are wise. . . . We are weak, but you are strong" (1 Cor. 4:9-10). His irony was designed to expose their folly.

The Corinthian congregants had adjudged their founding pastor as unwise, lacking insight into human nature, and fool-hardy in practicing his vocation. So the apostle gently confronted their false wisdom and imagined power. They, not himself, were arrogant judges of character in criticizing God's servant. Theirs was the same logic a family member or friend might use today to dissuade a young medical missions volunteer: "But you could make so much more money doing surgery in America!" Indeed, vocational Christian workers appear "fools for Christ's sake."

Consider Dan, an executive in the United States steel industry, for example. He was impressed through spiritual renewal to become more active as "an ordinary layman" in his church. When involvement in church offices excited him to study theology and understand church polity and programs, Dan responded to God's call to become a minister. He and his wife visited seminaries and selected a school. He resigned his position and moved so that he might begin seminary studies immediately. Dan's initial perception of ministry was the pastorate. Experiences in small churches as a student pastor and the school curriculum convinced him he was better suited in religious education.

Reflect on experiences of three women in ministry whom we shall call Betty, Ann, and Sherry. Reared in Christian homes in areas as diverse as California, Arkansas, and Texas, while growing up, each woman had served as a volunteer in her home church. The nature of their steps to salvation and personal callings to follow God took them across different frontiers. Betty and Ann married a minister and dentist, respectively, and found themselves serving as missionaries in East Africa. Ann is the mother of three children and Betty of five. Designated "church and home" workers in career assignments, they have claimed diverse ministries within their mission family and with African nationals in their adopted country.

Sherry, on the other hand, is a candidate for the Doctor of Philosophy degree in a Southern Baptist theological school. The daughter of a schoolteacher mother and government-employee father, she is a gifted thinker and writer. Ordained to Christian ministry after completing the Master of Divinity degree, Sherry has pioneered an associate pastoral ministry with an upper middle-class, urban congregation. Now approaching the completion of her doctoral dissertation, Sherry faces a new career decision. Shall she seek a pastorate and care for God's flock, a professorship and instruct seminarians, or a clinical appointment as chaplain in some hospital's department of pastoral care? If none of the above, what then? Shall she remain single or marry? Such decisions are inescapable as she faces challenging responsibilities in Christian service.

Stan is a former professional football player and seminary graduate who has found fulfillment in prison ministry. Walter, a native Midwesterner, has worn half a dozen different hats in diverse ministries: associate pastorates in two metropolitan churches, founding pastor of a mission church in the Northeast, single term missionary appointee as teacher in a Third World country, counseling center director, and coordinator of retreat center programs. He and his wife are recognized as sensitive, talented people on mission. They have sought to proclaim the good news of God's love, mid numerous settings, in imaginative and constructive ways. Consider still another caregiver.

Harry has maintained a lower profile than either Stan or Walter during his ministry career. Like them, his roles have undergone continuous metamorphosis: small church pastorates, campus student ministries director in a large state university, associate pastor of a major metropolitan church, visiting seminary professor, and now pastor of a thriving suburban congregation. Harry and his schoolteacher wife have lived full circle; their eldest child will soon become a seminarian! They have sampled Christian service opportunities like a smorgasbord buffet and learned the theological significance of Christ's words: "Greater love has no man than this, that a man lay down his life for his friends" (John 15:13). Now in his forties, Harry faces mid-life questions like: Is *that* all there is in ministry? and, Where can I make my life really count for God in the years I have left?

Ministers and missionaries like Dan, Betty, Ann, Sherry, Stan, Walter, and Harry would call themselves ordinary people on the journey of faith. Sometime, somewhere, somehow they each took personally the "Go" of the Great Commission. God's private call, received in the secret places of the heart, was confirmed in what John Calvin described as "the external call" —approval by "the public order of the church." Thereby, they became people on mission.

It is for caregivers like these that Christian laymen are themselves called to care. Rather than shrinking back from them, churchmen at their best join such servants of God as fellow priests and proclaimers of truth. The apostle Peter expressed such commonality in mission thus: "You are a chosen race, a royal priesthood, a holy nation, God's own people, that you may declare the wonderful deeds of him who called you out of darkness into his marvelous light" (1 Pet. 2:9). God's people ideally are not divided into opposing camps of clergy and laity, the leaders and the ones being lead. Rather, they are all on mission to win to faith people estranged from God. They form a special network of people who care.

We have seen there is no one single way of becoming a Reverend or of doing Christian ministry. If ministers and missionaries were tailors, the garments they fashioned would be like Joseph's coat of many colors. To pursue the analogy of tailoring, ministers' daily fashion creations appear more as bits and pieces of multicolored material in imperfect garments than custom-crafted costumes and clothing. Christian helpers cannot control life's human factors.

To appreciate more fully people who pursue God's call in some expression of religious vocation, let's consider a typical week in the life of one minister. Such a slice of life may provide a road map for understanding challenges, opportunities, and heartaches of persons whose life-style is obedient service, not just a church "job."

Six Days Till Sunday

Laypersons see ministers scrubbed and well groomed on Sunday, their faces brightened by the love of God. Hymns of faith from the choir and congregation fill the sanctuary with music. Challenging words from the Bible inspire devout worshipers to do God's bidding. But what happens on Monday, when the brightness on the pastor's face begins to fade? The sermon theme loses force, music stops, lights go out; the fire and majesty of worship celebration turn to ashes. For a minister on Monday morning, it's always six days till Sunday. What is it like to wear clergy garments or walk in a Christian helper's shoes? I want to share the minister's heartbeat with you.

Rather than respond from fantasy, pretense, imagination, or wishful thinking, I shall share what a typical week looks like from a seminary teacher's perspective. In relating my story, I remember others in religious vocations—students of both sexes and all races now preparing for ministry as pastors, church musicians, business managers, chaplains, educators and recreation specialists, social workers and counselors, institutional administrators, agency executives, missionary specialists in homeland and overseas assignments, seminary and university professors, television programmers, journalists, creators of Christian literature, computer technicians, and church office personnel. Each of these workers in vocational religious callings, of all Christian denominations, serves as one strand in the ecclesiastical web of life. They interface frequently with millions of competent laypersons, nonordained volunteers in the churches, in obedience to Christ's command to be his witnesses in Jerusalem, Judea, Samaria, and to the ends of the earth (Acts 1:8).

Day One.—I awakened at 4:30 AM because of an early morning plane flight to serve as consultant to a hospital's clinical pastoral education program. It's a forty-five minute freeway scramble to the airport. I boarded about 6:40 AM and checked student reports received the previous day while enroute. Jim, the department staff member who met the plane, is in his thirties and a doctoral degree seminary graduate. He and his wife of more than a decade were divorced after years of hurtful misunderstanding. Jim has remarried and is learning to partner and parent in a blended family confirguration. He has known days of anguish as well as hope.

One after another, the student chaplain trainees came for evaluation interviews—young to mid-aged, Latin and Anglo, male and female ministers. Their life stories were marked both by blessing and curse from childhood. Their faces revealed high idealism and the pain of false starts in religious vocation. None is without courage. Several of them, however, lack vocational clarity. In a few months, they will be graduated and poured like a waterfall over the edge of educational threshold into the ministerial market pool.

The evening was spent at dinner with a longtime friend and his wife. He is a distinguished clinical educator, past-president of the College of Chaplains of the American Protestant Hospital Association. She is a registered nurse. They have two grown sons and two grandchildren. They were planning for a month's teaching mission in Durban and Port Elizabeth, South Africa. Each of them will lecture to laypersons and missionaries in the area of family life and health. Having returned recently from Johannesburg and Cape Town myself, I am their resource person. They are full of questions and needs for reassurance. It was an eighteen plus hour day.

Day Two.—Having agreed in advance to breakfast with a pastor friend whom we shall call David, he and I met at 7:20 AM. The Holiday Inn buffet was too much food; we selected waffles instead. Our true *bread* was the inner workings of his congregation which is rebounding slowly from serious leadership mistakes made by his predecessor. The loves that lubricate his life include his Lord, his family, the church staff, and his congregation in that city. Bent one hundred ways between his pulpit work and denominational service plus many congregants requiring pastoral care, there's seldom time for play. Now in his early forties and a part-time teacher, David's identity as minister has not yet come clearly into focus.

More clinical pastoral education student evaluations that day reflected a mix of certainty and wistfulness in the candidates. They do want to serve God with heart, mind, soul, and strength in a focused way. But they wonder about finding freedom for themselves mid congregational expectations, scarcity of support groups for sharing concerns, and financial security in a roller coaster economy. These novices in ministry face baffling issues in their struggle to be human.

Audrey, a thirty-seven-year-old single, female chaplain trainee, transported me to the airport. A Master of Divinity seminary graduate, she had worked previously as a bank teller and as a missions volunteer with the African Inland Mission in Kenya. Audrey wondered whether or not her denomination is taking significant strides toward accepting women into the ministry. Reflecting Christian humility and feminine reserve, she was in an involuntary holding pattern concerning placement. How should Audrey assert herself? She and I explored some appropriate ways for making herself known and available. Though key ministry opportunities for theologically educated women are rare, they are real and growing in number.

Back in Fort Worth that evening, my wife and I accompanied a retired postmaster friend—widowed eighteen months earlier —to dinner, then back to our home for a visit. Married over fifty years, his late spouse contracted hepatitis and died slowly over a ten month span. Tears still flooded his eyes as he continued the work of grieving with trusted friends. Though weary, I felt it terribly important to befriend one still adjusting to the shock of death.

Day Three.—Furloughing missionary candidates, some of whose experiences Gloria and I shared in three trips to Africa, had convened in Dallas for a debriefing and reentry seminar. One of our mission board family specialists, Truman S. Smith, spent part of a day and night with us. Truman lost his first wife by death. After a wintry period of anguish, he remarried. Now, Truman and his nurse-wife and children model Christian family life at its best. The Scriptures report of Saul's son Jonathan that he "strengthened [David's] hand in God" (1 Sam. 23:16). That could be said mutually of our family's friendship with Truman and Gwen. We have shared programs and travels, talked, laughed, hurt, prayed, healed, and grown together in mutually enriching fellowship.

There was a wedding announcement tea that afternoon. The son of ex-missionaries (now faculty colleagues) was marrying a young lady from Michigan. He is a radio announcer; she a bookseller. How right it all seemed to start life over in the springtime with young love.

Later that day, my wife and I visited my mother who recently had moved into a retirement center. A few weeks before, she courageously left her central Louisiana home of sixty years to come back to Texas. As a teenager she had attended Mary-Hardin Baylor, then a woman's college, in Belton, and had come to appreciate the Lone Star State. Giving up her role as a retired educator and respected historian in Pineville and Alexandria, mother chose to return to her adopted state and be near part of her small family.

Day Four.—Today marked the beginning of an annual Christian Life Commission workshop on campus, this one probing family issues. Workshop leaders explored topics on the spiritual foundations of the family, character development, family relationships, and ministry with families. It was a time to renew acquaintances and profit from reflections of fellow presenters since I was to address plenary group sessions the next two days. Preparation had required weeks of work.

Day Five.—Months before while I taught pastoral care in Limuru, north of Nairobi, Kenya, during a sabbatical leave, an invitation came from the Texas Christian Life Commission staff. They wished me to address the theme: "Theological Foundations of Family Life." I had poured myself into the African mission adventure the prior six months—a different world from the West. Thus, preparing to discuss sensitive family issues during the weeks prior to the workshop challenged me to grow. I felt my presentation of "Partnership: A Christian Interpretation of Marriage" should reflect a "radical middle" view for that audience.

Day Six.—The workshop concluded. Involvement in such events provides a way to learn from one another. My address, "The Role of Parents in Parenting," was well received but rushed. The presider cut fifteen minutes from the schedule which left no time for audience response. In a closing musical parody of the workshop, composer-artist Ken Medema imagined entrees on a menu at the "CLC Restaurant." With a touch of genius, irony, and class, Ken helped presenters feel that they had contributed something worthwhile to a feast on family concerns.

That morning, Gloria and I shared an hour's coffee conversation with a pastor friend whose son will enroll soon in Southwestern Seminary's Master of Divinity degree program. "Be to Jeffrey, Doc, what you were to guys of my generation," he said with a twinkle in his eye. Now in his third major building program, the man is weary of committee meetings, high finance, and construction crews. He would like to be an ordinary minister instead of a program promoter.

Day Seven.—The telephone rang before dawn Sunday morning while I was still asleep. "This is Martha Weaver," the caller identified herself. Martha's father, a well-to-do businessman, had had a severe stroke seven months earlier. Hospital personnel had called the family before 6:00 AM reporting a deterioration in Mr. Weaver's condition. Martha called me since her pastor was out of the city, along with close relatives and friends. Her father appeared to be dying.

That day I drove 260 miles, round trip, to the hospital caring for my friend, Noble Weaver. Terry, his son from Dallas, rode with me. The specter of death was unsettling. Doctors explained that Noble had had another secondary stroke early that morning. Three injections of Valium were required to sedate him. I entered his room with the family, saying nothing beyond a hushed greeting.

"Where does it hurt, Dad?" inquired son Terry.

"All over," came Noble's muffled reply. Life support tubes hung into and out of body orifices. He lay awake, eyes half closed, twisting under the bed linens in a dance of death.

The afternoon overtook us. Lillian Weaver showed all the strain of seven months of frequent travel from home to hospital, with nerves stretched thin by double messages from the medical staff.

"He might live one day, or he might live a year," the doctor said. We talked in hushed tones in the hospital cafeteria. Her faith in God had faltered through the long ordeal. Understandably, things just did not seem fair to her.

One of my parting acts of ministry was to heed Lillian's request for a moment of family prayer. We bowed in utter humility of spirit, clasping hands with her husband. What would I say? My words tried to fathom the impact of a doctor's prediction: "Mr. Weaver will not leave this place (alive)." I prayed for them gifts of courage and patience and the will to endure. A hug seemed the best way to say good-bye before Terry and I drove north toward home.

Six days till Sunday, indeed! The week was mine under God; yet, as his servant, I belonged in vulnerable ways to the world. Any yes one gives to inquiries, invitations, or requests from others becomes a blank check to be honored eventually at the bank called Time. In religious vocation, one's time, energy, and talents are the coin of the realm. What qualities characterize one who uses one's personality as a "fool for Christ's sake?"

The Intimate Life of Career Caregivers

Career ministers and missionaries live by their survival instincts, spiritual sensibilities, professional competencies, religious disciplines, and learned rules of thumb. Their duties come like a thousand pieces of building material which must be collected and constructed into a sturdy house of faith. Like the honest physician who uses a blend of science, experience, and educated guesses in diagnosis, the Christian minister uses all he or she possesses in God's service for mankind. To understand career caregivers, the layperson might view them as being aware of God, in the family of faith, people on mission, disciplined professionals who are quite ordinary people. Let's examine these qualities in brief detail.

Aware of God

The Old Testament prophet Samuel is reported to have heard God's voice as a child. Born in answer to his mother's prayers and dedicated by Hannah to the Lord before his birth, Samuel was taken to Shiloh to be trained by Eli, the priest. While still a lad, he experienced a remarkable call to religious vocation and became a spiritual leader in a land where there was "no frequent vision" of God (1 Sam. 1:24-28; 3:1-18). Like Samuel of old, persons in ministry vocations are extremely sensitive to the voice of God.

Let's note characteristics of men and women in ministry whom you have met through these pages. Several of them were marked by a deep hurt, major loss, or psychic upheaval from youth up. We saw a loved one's death, divorce in the family, continuous career evaluation, extended singleness, culture shock of overseas residence, involuntary stresses at work, sex discrimination, and vocational instability. Reared for the most part in traditionally religious homes, their character development revolved heavily around life's *oughts.* Eager to please authority figures (to "amount to something" in life), they learned in practice about Freud's "obsessive-compulsive" personality type. At least some of them knew more of guilt feelings and inadequacies than of unqualified acceptance and affirmation from family members and persons in authority.

The ministry gains power and depth through an ordination from above. While career orientation and placement surveys steer many persons seeking vocational guidance, the minister's eye scans a different evaluation inventory. His or her fine tuning searches heaven and earth for God's work assignment and ultimate approval. Christian calling must be sorted out mid many choices. Such vocation resides in a sense of purpose for one's life that is not self-created. Given such confidence in God's intention for life like John Wesley, "the world becomes one's parish."

People in religious vocations are always in process. Not unlike persons in secular callings who lack vocational clarity, some ministers go to the ends of the earth to find their own souls. Their aspiration and independence soon collide with concrete realities, institutional guidelines, and historical limitations. The love of God they represent must connect with real people in untidy situations. Caught up in the success syndrome of making it in the Western world, failure is perceived as the unpardonable sin. Paradoxically, they know by heart that the peril of "having it made" in the religious realm is spiritual death.

Religious workers thus need true support groups because of the loneliness of their pilgrimage toward life's "impossible dream." They must hold ethical tension taut toward God's holy purpose while dwelling in unholy places. One hand holds the life of salvation in God's kingdom while the other computes church budgets, teaches English as a second language, conducts seminars for newly blended families, and pours oil on the troubled waters of some squabble. What an audacious calling! Fortunately for one's own good, the servant of God is a member of the "household of faith" (Gal. 6:10).

In the Family of Faith

The term *family* (*patria*) appears only once in the New Testament in Paul's doxology to the Father, "from whom every family in heaven and on earth is named" (Eph. 3:15). We may observe that members of the family of faith function as relatives for vocational religious workers—an essential social system in life.

The psalmist David, who lived a thousand years before Christ, wrote: "God gives the desolate a home to dwell in" (Ps. 68:6). It is also translated, "God setteth the solitary in families" (KJV). By way of application, I wish to focus on the need for family membership for the minister or missionary and members of their households. Without people upon whom they can truly rely, dependency needs sicken or surface in weird ways or go unmet. Without trusted friends in the "household of faith," the pastor and his wife will turn outside or go underground for befrienders. And a missionary's needs for community will be met by someone, for good or ill. This is especially true for single persons in overseas settings who need the warmth of people reaching out to them.

Particularly, since professional caregivers are community outsiders at work by invitation to a given place, local Christians need to reach out and support them. They bear the Father's name. Surely, he wants for them "a home to dwell in" so they will no longer feel desolate. God senses each person's need for strength "in the inner man" and sets himself the task of giving spiritual care (Eph. 3:14-16). Can His own people do less for one another in the human realm?

What do healthy families do for their members beyond receiving them as fresh gifts from God's hands and caring for them on the way to maturity? Kinsmens' hearts are trustingly open to each other. They teach and nourish one another— provide food, safety, and comfort, and give companionship on the journey of faith. Church family members ideally try to "live in harmony with one another" (Rom. 12:16), "love one another with brotherly affection; outdo one another in showing honor" (v. 10). That much we know to do.

Part of the skill of becoming *family* to caregivers is learning how to "rejoice with those who rejoice" and "weep with those who weep" (Rom. 12:15). I have referred earlier to weddings and divorces among religious workers, to births and deaths, to sin (however pious) and forgiveness, to unwanted singleness, to a woman's frustration in not finding a place of ministry, to eighteen-hour workdays, heavy travel schedules, nights away from home, occasional feelings of rejection, and endless calls for help. Ministers must occasionally pull up by the hearth, slip off their shoes, and probe the meaning of what they are doing with trusted friends. Laypersons can provide such centers of warmth and faithful feedback. Dare we withhold support and goodwill from caregivers who are on mission for God?

People on Mission

Persons in religious vocations have been characterized as being sensitive to God and as needing a supportive family network. Like their Savior, they feel a sense of chosenness and obligation to share His saving ministry with people sitting in darkness (Matt. 28:19-20). They are partners in Christ's global ministry and sense that without Him they can accomplish nothing (John 15:1-6). Given God's power, His servants can challenge any frontier, cross any barrier, and face any obstacle in reaching people who do not know about God.

Laypersons' partners in mission are more than professional church craftsmen. They are, as Wayne E. Oates once said, *professing* professionals. Their faith in Jesus Christ is affirmed though it may sometimes waver. His Word for them is "good news" to share. The nature of their work is a walk, a life-style, a journey of faith, a calling to follow the God who leads His people. Anyone who desires to share the ministry of a caregiver must understand the caregiver's deep sense of calling to evangelism, discipling, and Christian mission.

Disciplined Professionals

Christian ministry as a vocational arena runs the gamut of polarities: life and death, obedience and sin, belief and unbelief, grace and judgment, love and sexuality, providence and trust, divine mystery and human story. Its diversities know no limits; its duties are inclusive, from the ridiculous to the sublime. There appears to be room in ministry and missions for all sorts of folks: scholars and clods, prophets and clowns, mystics and materialists, saints and showmen, thinkers and activists, visionaries and provincialists, experts and bunglers, high achievers and goof-offs. Some ministers major on *being,* others on *doing.* Most of them resent being viewed as goody-goody (that is, affectedly good) for God. They want to be genuine men and women of faith.

The disciplined Christian caregiver is a true professional

person. He or she is educated in the language, lore, doctrine, and history of the church. Fine tuned in interpersonal relations, one quickly detects aberrations of the human spirit like: the deceptive, manipulative, angry, depressed, seductive, or emotionally ill individual. The professional worker belongs to a community of colleagues and is usually examined, licensed, certified, or ordained into one's calling. Such a skilled person does not rely upon charisma alone to underpin ministry but seeks full competency as a teacher sent from God (see John 3:2).

You will sense the time management skills required for speaking engagements, worship leadership, committee meetings, calls for help; study in preparation for sermons, addresses, and writing; mealtimes with family and friends, telephone calls, airport runs, requests for counseling, ad infinitum—described above in a typical week's work. There was not adequate provision for play, physical fitness, family relaxation, or spiritual development. To stay sane, one must discipline the disordered activities of life and, thereby, gain order over time. Above all, one must take time for God. While you cannot control your minister's fully human existence, you can encourage a comprehensive schedule which fosters wholeness and holiness. Remember, the religious professional is an ordinary person.

Ordinary People

We began our discussion by describing Christian caregivers as ordinary people in extraordinary callings. They are born, mature, marry, make love, become parents, get angry, miscalculate budgets, enjoy good humor, get speeding tickets, occasionally oversleep, have accidents, become ill, face surgery, age, and die like other human beings. Furthermore, they experience the seasons of life—from joyous celebrations to tragic crises—with their own family, close friends, church members, or mission "family." Even as they share the incomparable good news of the gospel with others, ministers recognize they "have this treasure in earthen vessels, to show that the transcendent power belongs to God" and not themselves (2 Cor. 4:7). Genuine humility is their daily bread.

Just because a church staff member or missionary has problems does not mean he or she is useless in Christian ministry. I recall a pastor who has served three congregations over a span of thirty years. Disappointedly, one of his children was involved in drug abuse at one stage of life. Another child had a serious malignancy which required extensive surgery and chemotherapy for a period of years. Life was not a wasteland for this friend, but neither was it a party. His churches, fortunately, have stood with him. To celebrate years of faithful service, his present congregation sent him on a study leave to a noted divinity school. Sensing how the years grind down a minister and his wife with the acids and abrasives of life, the congregation provided for his continuing education and pulpit supply during his absence. In such realistic ways, churches and denominational groups faithfully undergird the ministries of ordinary people.

To summarize, the layperson who would understand and seek to prize God's chosen servants may view them as people on mission, required by the very nature of ministry to live disciplined lives, and engaged in a fully human existence. It is a mutual priesthood they share in building a "spiritual house, . . . acceptable to God through Jesus Christ" (1 Pet. 2:5, 9-10). Persons in religious vocations are *people*, with all the rights and privileges of being human.

Ministers may feel themselves "fools for Christ's sake," with Paul's healthy sense of irony, yet press on. But the coin has another side. One thoroughly disillusioned in religious vocation might feel anguished, empty, devastated, and bitter. With that possibility in mind, we turn now to the idea of blessing or feeling good about oneself in ministry.

2 Blessing:
Feeling Good About Oneself

Christian ministry, correctly understood, is a collaborative enterprise between ministers and fellow believers. Their relationship is more like a family, ideally supporting its members, than a hierarchical organization. Membership in a church or mission family system creates images of ties that bind in Christian love in a community of trust and affirmation. Experiences in families remind us of the importance of "being there" with persons who need care in their efforts to achieve wholeness and holiness in life. Much of the anguish and heartache of leader-follower conflict in congregations would be eliminated by a mutual covenant between members and ministers to care for one another through all life's struggles.

The Bible reminds us that we can become available to each other in acceptance and encouragement because God is available to us. You may recall Jesus Christ's graphic imagery in a farewell discourse with His followers of Himself as the real vine and themselves as fruitful branches (John 15:1-10). Productive living was possible, Jesus said, to the degree they remained grafted into the Father's love. Such productiveness includes *being* God's people and *doing* His work. Nurture and mission thus proceed hand in hand.

In a dramatic forecast of His own sacrificial death, Jesus noted: "There is no greater love than this, that a man should lay down his life for his friends" (John 15:13, NEB). Then our Lord blessed His followers by designating them as His friends, no longer mere servants. He had disclosed to them all that the Father had revealed to Him; whereas, they were reminded, "The servant does not know what his master is doing" (John 15:15). Thereby, the Savior confirmed each follower in his own being with an eternal yes to any question about his worth in God's kingdom. The disciples had been observers of a drama of redemption. Soon, their participation in that drama would become total.

What Jesus did to fortify His followers for their ensuing mission, one's own and extended family members must do for today's ministers. It is a paradox, but ministers in one's religious support group must be nurtured themselves in order to survive, thrive, and serve. Christian leaders and followers need each other.

Here is a pastor, Jim we shall call him, an only child of parents who both were youngest in the sibling order of their respective families. Having never "made it" in their own eyes, his parents were dogged by feelings of personal failure. Distressed by their own faults, they gave more criticism than warm affirmation to their son. For years Jim secretly longed for a yes, a blessing, from significant persons that would enhance his self-esteem. He lived with a low-grade depression and more than his share of anxiety because of feelings of powerlessness.

"I feel impotent to make things happen as a leader of my congregation," Jim lamented. "People see me more as a warm listener than as a strong leader, able to motivate them in doing ministry." How he needed affirming, durable relationships with laypersons to counteract the chilling effects of a self-critical spirit.

Were Jim your pastor, would you like him to feel good about himself? How would you recommend that he enhance his self-image and strengthen his self-esteem? Jim's mentor proposed a professional career evaluation and mid-course correction majoring on his strengths. In order to understand more about the idea of blessing and development of self-esteem, let's look at the biblical idea of blessing—the gifts of delight, worth, value, power—given by parents to their offspring. Then we shall examine the significance and sources of blessing for Christian caregivers, and how we might enhance the esteem of ministers we know.

The Biblical Idea of Blessing

Blessing in the biblical sense implies the gift of power, potency, ability to generate, or contribute to bringing newness into being. Such generativity might contribute new human life or ideas, create new institutions, or provide fresh force for familiar causes within the stream of human history.

The ancient idea of family blessing parallels the modern notion of enhancing another person's self-esteem, so that one develops a clear sense of identity, worth, and value. The late Jewish thinker Martin Buber once observed, "Man wishes to be confirmed in his being by man, and wishes to have a presence in the being of the other. . . . Secretly and bashfully he watches for a Yes which allows him to be and which can come to him only from one human person to another." Such blessings are bestowed by significant persons rather than earned or merited. They are life's yes which encourages and frees one to be one's best.

Blessing in the Bible refers foundationally to the Heavenly Father's graciousness toward His elect people: Israel. Even as Abram was called, entrusted with a household of servants, sparkled upon with wealth and privilege, and marked by circumcision, he experienced divine favor. He became the covenantee and God the covenanter of a gracious promise (Gen. 17:1-21). At age ninety-nine, when Sarai, his wife, was ninety, God continued to promise Abraham a child of blessing. Isaac's birth thus continued the unique line of generations of persons who served God and ultimately pointed Israel toward the Messiah.

God's relationship with Israel became a paradigm of parents' joyous affirmation of their offspring. Given that model, the chosen people expressed delight in the birth of a child, especially a firstborn son, and a birthright blessing passed from father to eldest son (Gen. 27:1-30). Blessing implies warm acceptance into the family, but rejection casts a shadow of darkness into a child's life. One is under a curse. Whereas blessing prompts a child's sense of belonging, ability, specialness, and thanksgiving, curse prompts a cry of absence, anguish, loneliness, and impotence. The result is the difference between an "I can" and an "I cannot" existence.

Just as one's life comes from others, so blessing comes from another person. "When Abraham blessed Isaac," noted Myron Madden, "he passed his life to Isaac in a special way; the potency of the father was given to the son."[1] The blessing in this sense meant the father was expendable on behalf of the son. In turn, Isaac blessed Jacob in bestowing his being and power upon Jacob. Tricked out of his birthright, the twin brother Esau cried, "Have you not reserved a blessing for me?" (Gen. 27:36). But Isaac had bestowed his giftedness upon Jacob, and there was no turning back. The remnant of a blessing was received as a kind of curse, and Esau vowed to kill his brother Jacob. The incident points up the peril of family favoritism and need for fairness in gifts of family acceptance, affirmation, and provision for each child.

The Christian minister who lives and serves as a blessed individual has been welcomed into the world by parent figures who provided both security and a sense of belonging. An individual who accepts such affirmation matures in trusting relationships with members of the whole family, the larger community, and with God. In turn, he or she is freed to become a healthy, caring person who can pass on mutual respect and goodwill to others.

Some parents have no blessing to give, only a curse. Others care unwisely by holding on to offspring, meeting their own ego needs through dependent children, and never permitting them to cut loose. Still others abuse their children, so they become traumatized citizens of the larger world. Erik Erikson commented that some individuals marry to find their identity. Some alienated, star-crossed young people select the ministry as a vocation in a lifelong search for acceptance, identity, and security. Feeling fatherless, they wish for God to serve them as the warm, supportive parent they never knew. They may search with an almost pathological craving for approval, affirmation, and acceptance from a church or mission family. With feelings running the gamut from dependency to denied anger, such ministry candidates are high risks in the church. Accustomed to being evaluated, berated, or manipulated in continuing relationship patterns, they crave approval yet constantly fear rejection. Their anxious behavior may unconsciously invite the very criticism or rejection they dread.

Because a religious leader's self-image affects everything else —in the feeling, thinking, and behavioral realm—we shall note the significance of being a blessed person in Christian vocation.

Significance of Being a Blessed Person

A minister's leadership style gives clues to the presence or absence of self-esteem. Political scientist James MacGregor Burns wrote in a classic study entitled simply *Leadership* of dictatorial, transactional, and transformational leaders throughout history.[2] Adolph Hitler, who qualified as a negative model because of his dictatorial nature, was marred by paranoia, race hatred, and megalomaniac tendencies. Western leaders like Lyndon B. Johnson, Winston Churchill, and Franklin D. Roosevelt demonstrated the reciprocal mentality of transactionalism. They satisfied one good perhaps to achieve a larger good, made political appointments, and influenced legislation on the basis of calculated trade-offs. Whereas other leaders, like China's Mao Tse-tung, helped to transform their constituents' goals, values, decisions, and actions through majoring on end values like liberty, justice, and equality.

What is true of political leadership is paralleled in church and denominational history as well. One's self-image is a key resource to effectiveness in ministry. According to Webster, the noun *resource* is from the Latin *resurgere*—"to rise again"—akin to resurrection. A positive self-image ideally provides the available means or resources which enable a person to meet life's challenges.

An instrument designed to assist individuals in assessing their own self-esteem level contains ten statements.[3] The user evaluates each item with one of four alternatives: (a) almost always true, (b) often true, (c) seldom true, and (d) almost never true. The first six items are weighted in scoring with values from *one* for (a) to *four* for (d). The last four items differ with reversed weighting from *four* for (a) to *one* for (d).

The following statements provide a clue to one's self-perception:

1. When I face a difficult task, I try my best and will usually succeed.
2. I am at ease when around members of the opposite sex.
3. I feel that I have a lot going for me.
4. I have a very high degree of confidence in my abilities.
5. I prefer to be in control of my own life as opposed to having someone else make decisions for me.
6. I am comfortable and at ease around my superiors.
7. I am often overly self-conscious or shy when among strangers.
8. Whenever something goes wrong, I tend to blame myself.
9. When I don't succeed, I tend to let it depress me more than I should.
10. I often feel that I am beyond helping.

An examiner suggests self-scoring of the instrument. If, for example, the first six statements are almost always true in a respondent's experience, the score is low. If the final four statements are almost never true in one's experience, the score is low. A total score of ten, lowest possible on the scale, indicates a healthy self-perception. A total score of thirty or more indicates excessive self-criticism. Such low self-esteem in a Christian minister, for example, would interfere with relationships and impair confidence in leadership.

Persons who enter religious vocations without feeling blessed live with excessive anxiety. Several reactions to low self-esteem may become evident. One, persons lacking self-confidence try to screen out activities where they might fail—playing tennis or golf, for example, if they don't know the sport or making evangelistic calls if they fear personal rejection. Two, others put up a false front, hoping to convince people of their worth. They are experienced, however, as defensive or insensitive individuals. A third reaction is bragging, self-praise, or seeking acclaim from one's people. Such behavior invites criticism, ridicule, or mimicry—the opposite response from that desired. Four, some religious workers play it safe by avoidance of contact with people except in situations where they are in control. They may opt to stay in the study or out of town, practice an intense spirituality, read or write excessively, practice a hobby, or retreat into a fantasy world where they imagine themselves as worthy of praise. Five, still others assume a "prophetic" stance by evaluating social or religious causes, institutions, individuals, denominational groups, or doctrinal positions. Presenting themselves as defenders of a safe theological or pure ethical system, they thereby seek praise or power or both. Sadly, such critical individuals often lead lonely lives. They are cut off from people, some of whom might enhance their self-worth through friendship in shared ministry.

Laypersons recognize intuitively the unblessed religious worker who struggles for freedom from inferiority feelings. Sensitive, wise congregants have seen clues to low self-esteem before like: arrogance as a mask for insecurity and loneliness; aggression as compensation for real or imagined weakness; authoritarian leadership rather than trusting the process of group decision making; and acquisition of worth through political prominence or prestigious position within the denominational framework. Such evidences of basic insecurity carry enormous price tags, both for religious workers and their constituents.

Consider some specific observations about the significance of feeling blessed. *One, blessing is a desire for confirmation as a fully human person by significant others.* In his autobiography *The Struggle to Be Free,* pastoral theologian Wayne E. Oates notes his social shyness as a backward teenaged page in the US Senate. From a cotton mill background of poverty and parental rejection in South Carolina, his fellow pages in Washington, DC, belittled his appearance, made fun of his speech, and ridiculed his behavior.[4] Oates longed for peer acceptance but was rejected. He would have agreed with Hans Selye that "the common denominator of all man's . . . efforts . . . seems to be a striving, consciously or subconsciously, to earn good will and gratitude from one source or another."[5] In time, with considerable help —human and divine—this man has served as mentor and spiritual father to hundreds of theological students, young physicians, and religious workers.

Two, blessing is a need for affirmation of one's acceptance within the cosmic order. To feel like a motherless or fatherless child—because of abandonment, divorce, work, war, death, neglect, or abuse—in no way eliminates the human need for acceptance, security, education in family lore, and a place within a meaningful order of existence. There are few sufferings equal to the pain of feeling no good, unattractive, unwanted, misunderstood, trapped, worthless, rejected. In one six-week period, for example, five teenagers from homes in fashionable Westchester County, New York, committed suicide.[6] Feelings of powerlessness and worthlessness know no age, racial, economic, sexual, or national boundaries.

Particularly when human families and friends fail to understand someone, one often turns to heaven for help. They may look magically to God in weakness for strength, in shyness for certainty, and in loneliness for comradeship. The Christian community may offer spiritual parents and loving peers in lieu of what life lacks. For some persons, pursuing God's call in choosing a vocation seems a natural way to find ultimate acceptance, power, and meaning or success.

Three, closely related to acceptance is the longing for companionship on the journey of faith. The word *companion* is from two Latin words, *com* and *panis,* meaning "with bread" or sharing food together. When one is sure nobody wants him around, one pulls away from the healing presence of everyday human associations that persons who enjoy a sense of worth take for granted. Take Mark, for example, a young minister in his late twenties who lived with a gnawing sense of failure. While growing up, he had to produce, work part-time, and provide for his parental family without regard for who he was as an individual. Faced as an adolescent with an overwhelming sense of responsibility for his relatives' welfare, he experienced feelings of powerlessness, isolation, and failure. Mark carried his lonely, helpless feelings into adulthood, marriage, and ministry. As a consequence, he views the church as a potential band of brothers and sisters who will meet his dependency needs. He thrives more in terms of what they can do for him than what he might do for them in a community of faith.

Four, blessing acknowledges the universal desire for recognition and approval of one's giftedness and accomplishments. From life's beginning, whatever level of physical and mental ability one may possess, approval needs persist. A person requires recognition of gifts, education in the language and lore of his people, encouragement of initiative, praise for performance, and appreciation of contributions made to the human enterprise. Acceptance also includes challenge of errors, forgiveness of faults, and encouragement of efforts. Ministers and their families are not exempt from such needs for recognition and approval.

Remember that helping vocations are open to grievously handicapped persons like: paraplegics and quadriplegics with spinal cord injuries, visually impaired individuals requiring assistance themselves, and epileptics whose involuntary seizures are controlled by medication. Other ministers are *different* by reason of background like: divorce, a prison record, drug or alcohol abuse, emotional illness, or trauma of rape or war. Far from holding grandiose notions of themselves because of their uncommonness, such individuals are acquainted with deep grief, pain, and suffering. Their spiritual sensibilities are often more acute than nonhurting people. Here's the point. Whatever one's mental abilities, physical capacities, and emotional gifts, one needs recognition and approval from significant others.

Fostering a sense of blessedness is an important goal for home and church. Given supportive allies, teachers, and models, an individual's damaged self-perception can change. The awareness that one is accepted by God and respected by Christian friends fosters an optimistic outlook on life.

Developing a Sense of Worth

Persons who feel good about themselves are free to become involved in sharing the needs of others. Developing a sense of worth may require profound transformation. But how? You may recall the experience of Jacob at the Jabbok brook, wrestling with God's unnamed, special messenger (Gen. 32:22-25). Having lived deceptively with his uncle Laban and having tricked him out of flocks of animals and much wealth, Jacob faced a moment of truth with his conscience. As he struggled through the night in a divine-human match, Jacob plead for a blessing (Gen. 32:26-32). When morning came, he was wounded in the encounter, yet his prayer for blessing was heard. At

Peniel he received a new name: Israel, meaning prince of God; a new, more humble nature; and a new desire to serve Jehovah as he and his household returned to the Promised Land. Esau, the brother he feared because of previous deception in taking the birthright, appeared on the horizon in the company of four hundred men. They exchanged greetings and were reunited in tender forgiveness and mutual brotherhood (Gen. 33:4-17). In Jacob's experience, we may see further the significance of being a blessed person.

I have suggested that developing a sense of worth continues through the course of one's life. A person might feel good about himself in one period of years, then decompensate in mid-life or old age to feelings of worthlessness. Later, one's self-image might be providentially redeemed. Such was Jacob's case. The constellation of his experiences mirrors many ministers' stories today. With certain details of Jacob's life in mind, we may observe several things about the origin and enhancement of self-esteem.

First, feelings of personal worth are rooted in one's family and cultural ancestry. A child's self-perception comes with the territory of birth and life's chances. In some cultures, for example, girl children have not been appreciated as much as male descendents. Infanticide, taking the lives of unwanted offspring, has persisted in limited form throughout recorded history. Lives of infant females were snuffed out in ancient Rome. They are reportedly being killed, in rare instances, in the People's Republic of China today. In some nations women are viewed as property of their husbands or fathers. Such cultural adversity sabotages feelings of worth and interferes with relationships.

Years ago, I met Wilma Rudolph, a black woman from Tennessee and a world champion runner. As a child Wilma was burned severely, yet her mother medicated and massaged her legs for years. She was encouraged to walk, run, and play with other children her age. Rather than giving way to scarred skin

and memories of crippling burns on her legs, Wilma determined to "be the best." Her experience reminds us that self-
esteem is communicated within one's cultural and ethnic history. It is absorbed from one's national identity, as can be
observed in a rising tide of nationalism around the world.

Potentials for self-confidence and self-criticism cluster in
family interrelationships. Let's return, for example, to the
Genesis story. When Jacob obtained Isaac's blessing by dubious means, Esau's loss dramatically underscored the worth of
parental goodwill. Two sons, reared in apparently identical
circumstances, experienced parental favor in completely different ways. One moved through life as an insider, the other an
outsider. One felt accepted, the other rejected. Yet, as already
indicated, Jacob's pride and Esau's prejudice were both redeemed by the Heavenly Father. Ultimately, the alienated
brothers were reconciled, accepted each other, and dwelled
safely in the land (Gen. 33:12-20).

Second, one's self-image is both received and sought. Persons are in a
continuous process of becoming. One is what one has been
given by significant others and what one seeks to become by
conscious choice and strength of will. Along the way there is
much redoing of life's experiences. By that, I do not imply
merely a rearrangement of emotional furniture in one's house
of faith. What one determines to become, under God, is more
than a touch-up job. Small alterations may help some persons.
In other instances, however, it requires removing the rubble of
previous, perhaps defective, building materials and recon-
structing one's personality on a sturdier, more suitable foundation. That entails emotional reeducation with wiser models and
healthier mentors than one has known in the past.

We see women in ministry blessing themselves because their
search for affirmation and appropriate role models has been
frustrated in a male-dominated culture. Few women ministers
today have been taught by female theologians. The preachers
they hear and the literature they study reflect masculine voices

and perspectives. While the grasp of women's calling holds them firmly to vocational ministry, cultural attitudes and behaviors may block their satisfaction in employment.

A female leader addressed a conference for women in ministry by identifying real issues they face. "Because women ministers are few in number, we are an oddity in some people's minds. . . . Women simply do not fit the cultural stereotype image of minister."[7] Numerous challenges like the woman's role in her family, male social control, lack of female role models, placement, and blending of marriage, family, and ministry were posed for the conferees. "Considerable confusion abounds," she lamented, "when women express calling to a culture that has not the ears to hear it." Ordination of women in ministry has become a bitterly divisive issue that will be addressed, though not easily resolved, in church forums for years to come.

This leads to a third observation. *A Christian person's sense of worth is in the process of being redeemed.* One's self-perception involves a point in time and a lifetime process. Its formation is more like a motion picture than a single print—a continuing series of impressions, feelings, commitments, and decisions. Negative feelings particularly must be faced, worked through, and mastered. My use of "being redeemed" implies a change for the better—for constructive, creative living.

Writing of the salvation process, beyond conversion proper, Paul said to the Christians in Rome: "Salvation is nearer to us now than when we first believed" (Rom. 13:11). He had a distinct impression of the brevity of life and coming end of the earthly order of things they knew. Elsewhere, he wrote to dear friends in Philippi, "Work out your own salvation with fear and trembling; for God is at work in you, both to will and to work for his good pleasure" (Phil. 2:12-13). The journey of the human self requires mastery of old, faulty impressions and feelings like anger, jealousy, insecurity, and self-doubt. While such mirrors of oneself influence behavior negatively, they can be polished or reframed with true effort.

Blessing may come from a significant person late in life. An aging parent may move from neutrality or outright rejection to favor a son or daughter in religious vocation. Such was the experience of Zelma Pattillo whose eighty-five-year-old mother had always said, "You know women can't be preachers!"[8] Her turnaround came late, yet it came.

During a visit home, Pattillo's mother responded to a query about her minister daughter thus: "There are many gifts. She could be an enlightener." A middle-aged daughter had "ears to hear" and claimed her mother's reluctant approval. "One who enlightens," she mused later. "I will take it as my blessing!" Such affirmation may be savored where we find it.

Hang-ups may take one far from one's childhood family in a search for spiritual parents. Much money and time may be invested with members of the medical and educational professions to check on one's emotional and intellectual progress. Single ministers are particularly vulnerable to feelings of low self-esteem since they fail to fit the marriage mold of cultural expectation. One's covenant family can help a person face shortcomings or feelings of bondage to the past (that is, from a childhood family). Since singles have no spouse with whom to check out reality, a covenant bond with a spiritual family or soul friend may prove helpful. Chances are good that a church can provide befrienders for elevating or cultivating worth and encouraging productivity among Christian caregivers.

How to Encourage Ministers You Know

Ideally, the church in each of its expressions—local, denominational, and universal—is a repository of blessing. The local congregation's organization into small groups for education and service provides a natural support network for each member. The church at its best is an extended spiritual family for laypersons and ministers alike. It was his bond with other believers of sharing "the unsearchable riches of Christ" that led Paul to thank the Father, "from whom every family in heaven and on earth is named" (Eph. 3:14). The apostle gloried in the inclusiveness of the gospel that offered heirship to Jews and Gentiles alike in God's salvation plan of the ages. They were members together of the family!

I recall particularly how certain ministers, who were older than I, related to me as a beginning seminarian. At the time of ordination by my home church, the pastor was a scholarly man, astute in thought and respected in ecclesiastical circles. But he was emotionally aloof, cold, unable or unwilling to enter into my fright as a novice headed for my first student pastorate. When approached about the best set of commentaries he knew for one in the beginning phase of ministry, he proposed a set of books that proved virtually worthless to me. No gift Bible was presented to me on behalf of the congregation as was the custom during such a religious ceremony. Having been reared from infancy in that church, I was wounded deeply by such an oversight or omission. No supportive phone call or correspondence ever came from that man to encourage me in the start-up phase of religious vocation. Though I was orphaned at age nine and much in need of blessing, that minister had no gift to offer me.

Treatment at the hands of one of his predecessors, however, proved warmly encouraging to my wife and myself. An elderly, retired minister who had served as my deceased father's pastor during the depression era became a spiritual father to me. He and his lovely wife (who by then was crippled severely with arthritis) lived in a town near my second pastoral assignment. My wife and I visited them occasionally for fellowship and to learn what life was affording them in their senior years. Also, they graced us with their warm love, shared things "old and new from the treasures" of their wisdom, and provided needed friendship to young beginners in ministry. I thank God upon every remembrance of their tender care.

These contrasting men and events are sketched to belittle no one, only to remind you to encourage your minister and missionary friends along the way. "But how can I help?" you ask.

Personal Ministries

At the personal level, you may enhance a minister's self-worth in practical ways. *One,* get to know individuals in church-related vocations as *persons* not roles. Viewing oneself as "just an ordinary layman" and placing the pastor on a pedestal puts a great gap where a bridge should be. Christian ministry is a collective enterprise. "We are labourers together with God," Paul reminded the Corinthian Christians about ministry (1 Cor. 3:9, KJV). Relating to a religious leader can be a bifold tie—to the office one fills and the shoes one wears. Yes, you can respect the office: pastor, teacher, administrator, missionary. But you can relate to the individual as a warm human being.

Closely related, *two,* observe their human feelings, needs, special family events like birthdays and anniversaries and critical moments. What does a pastor's wife experience during her pregnancy, for example, when the women of the church relate to her as one of them—not an outsider? Their notes, small gifts, cheery phone calls, and honest answers to an expectant mother's questions all spell *we care.*

What does a missionary couple feel, for example, when their nine-year-old son is struck and killed by a vehicle on a street in Harare, Zimbabwe? Grief? Yes. Wonder? Yes. Anger? Yes. Mystery as to why bad things happen to good people? Yes, and more. To deny them access to their stunned pain, anguish, and sorrow, by expecting missionaries to relate bravely to death, leaves few doors open. Either they can deny the crushing hurt in their hearts by glossing it over, or they can make believe death did not happen by keeping the lad's image alive. Fantasy can be harder to face than fact. Such a couple may need financial support in returning the child's body to the United States for burial. They certainly need prayer support and letters of consolation.

This means, *three,* you use ordinary means to bless religious workers. Tools in your hands include positive regard, friendship, genuine praise when due, financial aid when it is needed, supportive correspondence, shared meals, enjoying celebrative events, providing useful gifts of books, clothing, equipment, and so on. One pastor and his wife were routinely stuck with the bill for meals out with friends. Though there was no hospitality fund provided in the church budget, parishioners assumed the young pastor had extra money for entertainment. Instead of being provided for periodically by gracious hosts, that ministry couple did most of the entertaining themselves. In short, give companionship on the journey to encourage and affirm persons whose entire lives are spent in caring for others.

Partnership Ministries

The Southern Baptist Convention's Foreign Mission Board has encouraged associations of churches and state groups to "partner" with a national Christian group overseas. Called Partnership Missions, the resources of many individuals and churches collectively undergird the life and work of missionaries and nationals in many countries. Not only is funding provided for church construction, growth thrusts, and enlarged ministries, laypersons themselves are encouraged to spend time as volunteers in overseas settings, using their gifts in cooperation with national Christians and missionary personnel.

My wife and I can testify to a fresh internationalism, spirit of ecumenical effort, and the transcending of racial and cultural barriers because of numerous opportunities to share ministry on other continents. Once an individual has given part of his or her life in international mission, the world is viewed through clearer lenses.

The above example of collective leadership and witness can be multiplied in terms of initial clergy preparation for vocation, health care, conferences, continuing education opportunities, annuity retirement provision, and the like. Where one person's resources may be quickly exhausted in the blessing process, shared care can prevail.

To summarize, we have said with Martin Buber that "man wishes to be confirmed in his being by man . . . a Yes which allows him to be and which can come . . . only from one human person to another." God's relationship of blessing with ancient Israel served as a model for biblical persons, even as it points the way for parental affirmation today. We have seen the significance of curse and blessing in human experience and explored pathways for developing a sense of worth in life. How you might help ministers you know feel good about themselves concluded this section. Next, we shall consider the crucial place of expectation in ministry formation.

Notes

1. Myron Madden, *The Power to Bless* (Nashville: Abingdon Press, 1970), p. 142. See *Claim Your Heritage* (Philadelphia: Westminster Press, 1984).

2. James MacGregor Burns, *Leadership* (San Francisco: Harper and Row, 1978).

3. Source unknown. See Merton P. Strommen's "Cry of Self-Hatred," in *Five Cries of Youth* (San Francisco: Harper & Row, 1974), pp. 12-32.

4. Wayne E. Oates, *The Struggle to Be Free* (Philadelphia: Westminster Press, 1983), p. 31.

5. Hans Selye in William Glasser, *Stations of the Mind: New Directions in Reality Therapy* (San Francisco: Harper & Row, 1981), p. xvi.

6. Tom Brokaw, NBC/TV Nightly News, Mar. 16, 1984.

7. Debra Griffis-Woodbery, "Women in Ministry: Identifying the Issues," *Folio* (Winter 1984), p. 1.

8. Zelma Mullins Pattillo, "You Know Women Can't Be Preachers!" *The Christian Century*, May 30, 1984, pp. 566-67.

3 Expectation:
Pushing Beyond Established Boundaries

Have you had the experience of being in a large hotel when the fire alarm system sounded, and protective doors in wing corridors automatically closed? As a precautionary measure, my wife and I familiarize ourselves with exit routes and fire safety instructions when residing as hotel guests. During one visit to a major American city, our hotel's fire alarm system was set off during a fierce rain-hail storm. Because a killer tornado had swept a destructive path through that city ten years previously, residents had cautioned us about storms in spring. Surprised by the warning, we exited our fifth floor room via the nearest stairway, our hearts racing with excitment.

At the lobby area, hundreds of hotel guests were milling around as the device screamed its eerie signal. None of us knew precisely what to expect. Hail and rain pounded the roof, automobiles, and parking areas. Firemen examined the building and fortunately found no flames, only a switch set off during the electrical storm. With the state of emergency passed, crisis behavior subsided, and routine expectations resumed. We had mobilized for fire—just in case such a disaster happened. It was good to relax while still sensing aftereffects of the emergency.

Our lives ride twin rails of expectation and accomplishment or anticipation and failure to achieve some objective. The common denominator for hundreds of hotel guests was emergency expectation of a fire. We were warned to prepare for the worst. The verb *expect* is from the Latin *exspectare*, "to look forward to"

53

with anticipation. While we certainly did not desire it, the possibility of fire was thrust upon us. On the other hand, more pleasant symbols in life invite us to envision or prepare for some positive occurrence. Young couples, for instance, anticipate joyfully the birth of their first child. Christians throughout the world, for example, anticipate Easter with a high degree of certainty and expressions of hope. After a wintry season of "death," renewed expectancy is triggered by thoughts of Christ's resurrection.

Here, we shall see how the mutual expectation of ministers/ laypersons and missionaries/nationals pushes them beyond established boundaries into the unknown. Ideally, the church is a community of faith and expectation—fashioned to foster hope. We shall note the risk of pursuing the American dream when wed to religious idealism. Next, we shall examine the interface of expectation and accountability in church-minister relations, then close by exposing the vulnerability of the clergy as the hopeful profession.

Community of Expectation

Expectant thinking runs deep in Christian experience. Have you seen the spirit of a congregation rise and flourish in anticipation of the arrival of a new pastor to serve in the midst of God's people? At the outset, pastors are called upon to shape and clarify their expectations for and from a congregation. In turn, a particular community of faith specifies its desired directions, resources, and concerns for the future. Creative juices flow in the exciting mix of newness for pastor and people. The congregation's anxious longing for new leadership is met in one who himself brings fresh vision and bright hopes for the future.

Expectation of pushing beyond present achievements is the seedbed of effective Christian mission. The "Go . . . make disciples" of Christ's Great Commission is alive with prospects for the future (Matt. 28:19-20). All the dreams of missionary and mission family flow together to accomplish God's purpose in a particular place. Such hopes embody a two-edged potential—for achievement and joyous gratitude or for failure and unhappy resentment. More likely, however, people on mission must settle for the in-betweenness of negotiated priorities, compromised desires, partial accomplishments, and modest victories.

In theological terms, the local church is the crucible of the kingdom of God. Its life rises and falls on the tide of human personalities blended in redemptive efforts for persons and society. The building materials of its ministry are simple and sublime—people and their dreams—"treasure in earthen vessels," as Paul expressed it (2 Cor. 4:7). Ministers and missionaries pursue their careers in such communities of faith and expectation. The church, in turn, must cradle Christian vision, foster creative imagination, and protect persons who are clarifying their expectations in life. Unfortunately, some dreams never materialize but are stillborn.

Our Lord modeled fidelity to His followers and durability of caring relationships in the Kingdom enterprise despite broken dreams. The apostle John noted the power of Christ's bond in mission with His disciples thus: "Now before the feast of the Passover, when Jesus knew that his hour had come to depart out of this world to the Father, having loved his own who were in the world, he loved them to the end" (John 13:1). His covenant was to love them no matter what—rivalry for position, betrayal by Judas, denial by Simon Peter, and cowardice by companions who followed at a distance en route to the cross. Ultimately, their obedience was kindled by His enduring care and power of life over death.

Pastors, missionaries, and their fellow believers dare be no less faithful to one another than was Christ to His followers. Indeed, however, there is risk in holding great expectations in the Christian calling.

Expectation and Disappointment

Religious idealism fused with a search for the American Dream leads many seekers down the "yellow brick road." The need to succeed infects the ministry as it does athletics, medicine, politics, banking, law, engineering, the military, manufacturing, transportation, telecommunications, and the blue-collar world. Persons in service vocations want to "be the best" in their callings, too, though their drives toward excellence may be more deficiency motivated, disguised, or denied than in the arts, entertainment, science, and the like. Pursuing God's call in a religious vocation does not guarantee that one shall be rich in financial terms. That is rarely the objective. Still, the American dream of always bigger, always better exerts a captivating magnetism on individuals whose vocation is ministry.

Milton once wrote: "The mind is its own place and in itself can make a Heaven of Hell, a Hell of Heaven." Persons in religious vocations tend to live in an idealistic—onward and upward—world. The rub comes as expectation joins hands with imagination to plan specific, howbeit spiritualized, church goals. Concrete objectives, like constructing or remodeling a worship center or installing a new pipe organ, are easier to visualize, finance, and achieve than are intangible spiritual growth or ministry goals. Transforming a congregation's attitudes, values, hopes, or mission objectives often faces formidable barriers. Laypersons, dead set on dead center, are not easily weaned from lifelong priorities or patterns of malaise, caution, or prejudice. A pastor's brightest hopes may give way to discouragement when stumbling blocks erode idealism. Expectation, faced with foot-dragging passive resistance or assaulted by active criticism, may dissolve into shambles of exasperation.

Cases come to mind of missionaries and ministers who, unsupported by friends when the chips were down, experienced serious setbacks. For some, a series of petty annoyances eroded goodwill; for others, interpersonal irritants inflamed negative emotions; for still others, cultural frustrations fanned stressful feelings. Ultimately, some "straw" resistance, criticism, crisis, or failure "broke the camel's back" of will. Crushed by angry feelings of abandonment, a minister's spirit may slowly break in resignation. One is ready to find a home for the heart where constituents have kinder hands, and enemies in "the household of faith" can face each other in caring honesty. Often, it is health's failure or happenstance half a world away from one's post that severs ties and reassigns God's servants.

A frustration of expectations may carry volunteer dormitory parents in a much-needed residence for missionary kids back home to the United States. Feeding, clothing, and disciplining third culture children whose parents are employed in mission ventures can be much more difficult than an idealistic lay couple might dream. Such experiences have become actual events in different parts of the world. Perhaps someone in a position of responsibility could picture to volunteers, in advance, the realities of guest residential life among lively teenagers in a foreign city. Could consultation by a support committee of peers within their mission help them cope with disappointment? In some instances, volunteers are replaced by skilled career appointees. Seeing such floundering aspirants off at the airport does not help them sort out the emotional fallout of broken dreams. Once back in their home setting, it may take them months to make sense of what went right and what went wrong.

The absence or dissolution of one's support community within a congregation may contribute to a minister's loss of courage. A young pastor and his wife had relied upon the warm friendship of a middle-aged couple—Milt and Betty Rainey—in their church. Though considerably older than their pastor, the Raineys' acceptance had assured his reception by the city's inner circle of leaders. The Raineys had lived with

Betty's bout with serious illness for several years. One day after work in deep depression over her unwellness Betty took her own life, thereby beating death to the draw. Milt, a sensitive, somewhat stoical man, was crushed, angered, and mystified at being thus left alone.

Betty's pastor knew of her "dark night of the soul." They had talked of therapy for her despondency but not of suicide. As he prepared for and conducted a memorial service for his dear friend, the pastor's own spirit was bruised almost beyond belief. He and his wife faced in Betty's death the end of an era of supportive friendship. They sensed things would never be the same. Unconsciously perhaps, their reassignment to a new place of ministry had already begun. About six months after Betty's death, they moved to a challenging and caring congregation in another part of the country.

Former missionary Gladys S. Lewis has written of a disappointment of expectations she and her surgeon husband, Wilbur, faced in their adopted country of Paraguay. Poignantly, she traced their earlier years of finishing nursing and medical degrees, internship, residency training in surgery, military service, birth of a daughter and a son, and appointment as medical missionaries assigned to the Baptist Hospital in Asunción, Paraguay. A year at the Spanish Language School in San José, Costa Rica, preceded their arrival in a strange land.

> Finally, with our babies and with all our worldly goods in eighteen barrels and three crates, we chugged up the Paraguay River on a riverboat, en route to our destiny. We were . . . confident in the companionship of the One who called and sent us.
>
> There we were, trailing clouds of glory, to save all of Paraguay. To my surprise, crowds of Paraguayans did not meet the boat and fall down on their knees, begging me to tell them about Jesus. As a matter of fact, no one met us.[1]

Perhaps the mix-up in schedule and failure of any missionaries to serve as a welcoming committee was predictive of the ultimate inhospitality of that land.

After a decade of difficulties in seeking to qualify for a license to practice medicine in their adopted country, Paraguay's doors slammed shut. Three missionary physicians before them had traveled the road of split relationships between the Health Ministry, that granted permission to practice medicine, and the medical school, that offered the examinations leading to approval to receive a license, and had made it. "But we had come in a different time," lamented Lewis. "Nationalism was stronger. There were political in-house factors that did not pertain to us, but to which we fell prey and pawn."[2] Though Wilbur pursued every appropriate avenue of Spanish medical instruction and examinations by Paraguayan doctors, he was never authorized for official medical practice. His work of patient care was acceptable as long as he continued in the licensing process. Even that got squeezed by political pincers, and he was forced finally into hospital administration. When it became clear, after years of exasperating rejections, that Wilbur would not be permitted to do patient care, the Lewises decided to tell the mission they were leaving. Cutting loose from the people and place they loved and purpose of God, so clearly viewed years before, was unspeakably painful. But life has blossomed in beautiful ways for them back in the United States in the ensuing years.

These instances of frustrated objectives and inadequate support in the lives of God's servants could be multiplied a thousandfold. A minister husband's educated and talented wife may be discouraged from pursuing her own career because she is a woman and his wife. A missionary teacher may feel sinned against in his particular educational assignment without a community of scholars, in his field, with whom to exchange ideas. A young professor of religion actually resigned his appointment, with no job in hand, because his college's atmosphere was too stifling in leadership style and constrictive in theology. An associate missionary educator felt there was no need for his services because a capable national who spoke the vernacular language taught in the same field. The teacher's wife, a daughter of missionaries, had grown up in that particular country. While the foreign language and relations with nationals was "going home" for her, at his age it was culturally confusing and vocationally painful for him. So he resigned.

With the risk of broken dreams and crushing disappointments in mind, let us consider the nature of expectation and accountability in religious vocations.

Expectation and Accountability

Who actually is responsible for elevating expectations of ministers and missionaries? I have implied that both aspiration of ideals and the need to succeed go with the territory of religious experience in the United States. Children become bilingual in managing expectations of parents and teachers— attempt to please as God's persons and "make it" in a society of chronic consumption. We want *winners* at all costs. Hand in glove with winning is the public's outcry to "fire the coach" when the organization is not producing to their success standards. The hire-fire mentality of releasing employees in America's corporate world and replacing unsuitable representatives in our political system has infected the churches. The sacred has been secularized when Christians function more like corporate owners than members of Christ's body.

Concerning accountability, church executives and institutional employees are not as vulnerable to the public's touch as are front-line pastors whose tenure is less assured. Elected members of boards of trustees operate agencies and institutions in cooperation with employed executives. Missionaries appointed by a denomination's sponsoring board are in a more secure position, by far, than ministers and members of local church staffs.

One pastor jokingly said to a friend, "Do you realize we are always one Sunday away from being fired?" How do expectations and accountability work in the free church tradition?

First, consider a denominational agency, the Baptist Sunday School Board, which was established in 1891. Its basic program assignments are geared to serve the Christian education, Bible distribution, and communication needs of constituent churches. Prior to his installation as the Board's seventh president, Lloyd Elder was asked about his leadership style. He replied that he would like to participate in "servant-leadership or shared ministry" where the leadership and creativity of many persons work together.

"I want to invest my life . . . so that 1,500 dreams come true rather than having 1,500 people working to make my dreams come true," said Elder.[3] His formative image of administration is consultative direction under God's leadership. Since he expects to live up to an ideal of shared ministry, Elder must work to embody his vision in daily experience. Having served Baptist congregations as pastor over two decades, he appreciates the risky, faith venture nature of local church ministry.

Paradoxically, the same publication reporting Elder's tenure and expectations as Board president lamented the embarrassing dilemma of numerous forced terminations of church staff members in the denomination. "It is estimated that 2,500 Southern Baptist church staff ministers are dismissed annually," noted one speaker.[4] The problem of involuntary resignations leaves many ministers and their families emotionally and financially distressed, and churches frustrated and unstable. Supporting suddenly unemployed ministers and providing guidance for pastorless churches is taxing resources of church-minister relations directors from state conventions.

James Cooper, coordinator of the Ministers Counseling Service for the Baptist General Convention of Texas, observed that of a group of eighteen terminated ministers in his state, eleven received less than one month's salary. Furthermore, the average time for such dislocated ministers to find a new place of service, he said, is approximately eighteen months. (See Appendix 1.)

The church-minister relationship begins with a sense of God's guidance and blessing. Should not separation be surrounded with the same sense of God's leadership and approval? The calling process used by most churches imposes upon the congregation a profound covenant responsibility to support the minister and his family. Christian ethical considerations suggest that broken relationships be repaired in a spirit of forgiveness and fairness. If termination appears the best option for all parties, the congregation should continue the minister's salary and benefits for several months, or until the minister relocates. Such transitional support would avoid excessive stress and deprivation for the minister's family which often has no other source of income. (See Appendix 2.)

Prevention of church-minister conflicts is possible. Participants in a seminar exploring reasons for brief tenures agreed a frequent problem is that neither the church nor minister candidate knows what to expect in a new relationship. Expectations are seldom discussed in concrete terms. Both churches and ministers were seen as jointly responsible for brief tenures of service. Accountability should be accepted by both parties in the equation.

Alternatives to termination, such as counseling for the staff person or consultation for the church during a cooling-off period, were explored. With wise guidance from third-party leadership a church's ministry might be stabilized, its community influence strengthened, and a minister's career saved. Other solutions proposed were a more careful pastor selection process; improved communication between church members and ministers, with permission for criticism to enhance relations; personal-professional growth seminars for staff leaders; possible leave of absence; counseling; and use of known principles of conflict resolution. The need for some type of convenantal understanding, providing for negotiation and feedback, was suggested for ministers and congregations.

Jesus, being in "every respect . . . tempted as we are," faced a comparable situation to today's ministry (Heb. 4:15). His baptism at the hands of John in the river Jordan served as His commencement ceremony. God's voice introduced Him to all gathered friends, family, and future followers, "This is my beloved Son, with whom I am well pleased" (Matt. 3:17). What an impressive beginning! Then came Satan's scheme to challenge and undermine everything God had said about Jesus.[5] Had our Lord fallen into the trap of alternatives Satan presented, He would have failed to fulfill His calling.

In similar manner, when a seminary says to the churches, "Here is a servant of God whom we certify," lay leaders assume one is fully qualified. Baptists stand in the congregational tradition where one must candidate (try out) for a staff position. A church search committee may work through résumés of numerous candidates, a process which casts recent seminary graduates and seasoned pastors into competition with each other for the same position.

When I asked the chairperson of one pastor search committee about their progress, he responded: "We've worked through recommendations and dossiers of seventy-eight prospects and still have two more to go." That university city congregation had given itself a year, or longer if necessary, to find God's leader. In going to such a new place of service, the candidate wishes to be dealt with in an ethical manner.

Would it help you to understand more about the background and making of ministers? To know what is going on in the mind and heart of your church leader may help you to believe in what he is doing, pray for wisdom and courage during uncertain times, and offer support in life's ambiguous decisions.

Caring for the Caregivers

The Hopeful Profession

Those of us involved in the education of seminarians realize that we cannot assume a healthy spiritual background of wholesome family life for all ministry candidates. Certain ones of them bear scars of deep hurts from family alienation or misunderstanding. Some students are from dark backgrounds of sinfulness, not in touch with the shadow side of their mixed motives in Christian vocation. A few of them are profoundly confused and in need of emotional therapy. Other seminarians are from devoutly religious homes, but perfectionistic parents may have expected too much from a son or daughter. As a result feelings of guilt run deep, and self-esteem is lacking.

At a Personal Level

Personally, the Christian caregiver is a fellow believer, attempting to grow toward "the measure of the stature of the fulness of Christ" (Eph. 4:13). Minister Robert Raines wrote, in his late fifties, of the ambivalence he experienced when his seemingly indomitable father died in 1981. Reared in the vital heritage of a Methodist bishop's home, Raines became estranged from his father who was not easy to please. His *The Gift of Tomorrow* reveals a profound debt and enduring love for both his parents, particularly his late preacher father.[6] The book conveys his desire to preserve the world for coming generations as an expression of his own parental stirrings and strivings. Indeed, Raines has worked through mixed emotions to a latter-day peace within his own spirit.

Missionaries and ministers are human beings, subject to all the foibles and frailties of the flesh. They must learn to manage money, for they may have precious little of it after seminary graduation. Sexuality issues are pervasive. Single ministers are expected to remain celibate, chaste, and discrete in relationships with members of the same and opposite sex. Sexual fantasies, feelings, failures, and fears trouble married as well as single seminarians and may require attention at the hand of special counselors. Conflict plagues the minister's home where meaningful family time is sacrificed on the altar of multiplied religious activities. Inherited church problems, jealousy, and a desire for a life of one's own, quite apart from a ministry vocation, lead numerous spouses to make matters worse by divorce. Then, one's latter state is worse than the first because divorcees have frequently been excluded from ministry positions by cautious congregations.

Vast numbers of religious professionals are actually bivocational persons whose churches cannot afford to provide financially more than a partial salary. Time and money management are at a premium for the leader of the smaller church who works full-time in a secular position. Many bivocational pastors have not attended college and seminary. Yet the professional requirements in their churches for leadership skills, worship and preaching ability, and pastoral care wisdom may be quite high. Often, these bivocational pastors and their families attempt the nearly impossible by engaging in study programs as well.

It is difficult to imagine the personal struggles for faith, freedom, and fortitude going on behind the scenes in many ministers' lives. The tyranny of expectations may become overwhelming if professional duties and denominational program appeals fall upon someone already paralyzed with personal concerns. John Claypool confessed, in *Opening Blind Eyes,* to doing many right things for wrong reasons. As a youth, he bought into the philosophy that to *be somebody,* one must compete and achieve—even in pursuing God's call. Converted painfully from a life-style of acquisition to awareness, in 1976, he voluntarily moved from a pastorate of 5,000 church members to one of 450. Upon reflection he called it "the wisest move I ever made."

If "goddess success" failed to satisfy his spirit, what helped him, you wonder? Claypool said he found a new sense of worth by reexamining the biblical doctrines of creation and grace. He challenges church persons to open their eyes to two realities: "a true image of self," springing from the joyous intention of God in creation, and "the mercy that gives us life apart from our deserving—not once, but again and again."[7] One may be restored to a rightful mind in ministry by relearning oneself as declared worthy by none other than God.

At a Professional Level

Professionally, the Christian minister or missionary must demonstrate proficiency in the biblical, historical, theological, and functional areas of his or her calling. Seminaries' expectations of their students anticipate a product of autonomous (self-guiding), competent, and caring persons for ministry vocations. One school states the following objectives for students completing its required "Formation for Christian Ministry" course. At the close of their first semester, students should be able to:

Articulate the basic concepts of the Christian ministry.

Define the nature of their calling to ministry, their concept of themselves as ministers, and their tentative vocational goals.

Assess their readiness for ministry within the context of their tentative vocational goals.

Formulate growth goals to enhance their functioning as ministers.

Identify and demonstrate an understanding of the social and ethical demands of the Christian minister.

Utilize biblical, historical, theological, psychological, and sociological data to cultivate their images of themselves.

Develop an appreciation of the responsibility of the minister to be a peer support for fellow ministers by becoming a contributor to their fellow students' formation for ministry efforts.

Develop an understanding of the nature of the church and its mission as a context for ministry.[8]

Even a casual acquaintance with these requisites reminds thoughtful readers that ministers must continue to grapple with such fundamental issues for a lifetime. And this is only the orientation course for beginners!

As a professional person, the minister must understand fundamental theory, history, and skills in his or her area of major concern: pastorate, music, education, social work, missions, student ministry, communications, and the like. In a church or on a mission station one must be able to interpret the Scriptures with careful accuracy and apply them to actual life situations; to serve as worship leader and administrator in churches of unique social and ethnic context; to know how to select, train, and motivate volunteer workers in church settings; to negotiate philosophical differences and resolve conflicts with fairness and skill; to work as a member of a team (whether a church staff, educational institution, mission agency, etc.); and to keep clear about one's motives in all relationships in church, family, and society at large. Add to that, cross-cultural adjustments of persons in overseas settings, learning a second language, and transporting one's family and all one's earthly goods into another cultural-national context. Is there any wonder that expectations and accountability, before God and man, are such paramount issues?

Above all, what do ministers and their fellow workers understand that God expects of them as a called-out community of believers in the world? Determining His purpose requires prayerful openness to His Spirit's guidance and thoughtful negotiation of priorities.

Here, we have dealt with expectancy in the faith community as a primary characteristic of persons called and blessed in Christian vocation. Religious professionals have been viewed not as supersaints but as fellow strugglers who are committed to building a house of faith with their fellow believers. Disappointment casts its shadow of compromised plans and broken dreams into many lives, along with numerous spiritual victories. Lay leaders have been encouraged to foster hopefulness and protect persons who are clarifying their expectations in life. How pastor and people who are struggling with issues of expectation and covenant negotiate in actual situations has yet to be addressed. The need for security and satisfaction in ministry merits the separate discussion which follows.

Notes

1. Gladys S. Lewis, *On Earth as It Is . . .* (Nashville: Broadman Press, 1983), p. 4.
2. Ibid., pp. 179-87.
3. *Facts & Trends,* Feb. 1984, p. 9. See Lloyd Elder's keys to leadership in *Blueprints* (Nashville: Broadman Press, 1984).
4. *Facts & Trends,* Ibid., p. 10.
5. Ben Patterson, "The Wilderness of the Candidate," *Leadership* (Fall 1983), p. 20.
6. Robert Raines, *The Gift of Tomorrow* (Nashville: Abingdon Press, 1984), pp. 33,52.
7. John R. Claypool, *Opening Blind Eyes* (Nashville: Abingdon Press, 1983), p. 93.
8. Anne Davis and Wade Rowatt, Jr., eds., *Formation for Christian Ministry* (Louisville, Ky.: *Review and Expositor,* Southern Baptist Theological Seminary, 1981), pp. 9-10.

4 Place:

A Home for the Heart

A unique "given" of Christian vocation is profound restlessness experienced as the result of having no permanent place to call one's own. Like their spiritual father, Abraham, ministers and missionaries "sojourn in a strange land," hoping their children shall someday receive a permanent possession as an inheritance (Acts 7:5-6, KJV). *Place* may be used in several ways: physical environment, psychic space, particular spot, adequate room, or a proper niche for a person or thing. Our special usage here infers a home for the heart—a refuge from one's travels, respite from struggles, and a sanctuary where people are received and may find rest.

Jesus knew about having no people and no place of His own. Solitariness marked the lonely path of His redemptive purpose. "He came to his own home, and his own people received him not" (John 1:11). When grown, He left Nazareth but seldom returned to the home of His childhood. One observer recalled the Master, traveling along a road, joined by an enthusiastic, potential follower: "I will follow you wherever you go." But Jesus cautioned, "Foxes have holes, and birds of the air have nests; but the Son of man has nowhere to lay his head" (Luke 9:57-58). We can imagine Jesus pausing, fatigued along a roadside, at a well, or under the shade of a tree—but seldom at home. He did not crave an earthly place. The Bethany home of Mary, Martha, and Lazarus was a favorite sanctuary on His trips near Jerusalem. He was given no permanent place, prominence, or power by persons on earth. Our Lord's chief residence was in receptive human hearts (John 1:12).

Though God's Son experienced earthly homelessness, He remained undaunted because of His ultimate home with the Father. Jesus' profound sense of vocation kept Him in direct contact with another, larger Reality. Having no place and facing continuous criticism and conflicting expectations would have demoralized an inauthentic spiritual guide. Our Lord persisted in His mission of redemption on earth, anchored by single-minded devotion. Because he knew "that the Father had given all things into his hands, and that he had come from God and was going to God," Jesus faced His own death with spiritual strength and serenity (John 13:3). In today's terms, He was a risker with a purpose.

We may observe in this connection that Jesus Christ did not anticipate immediate acceptance or approval by His earthly parents, neighbors, and religious leaders who were slaves of orthodoxy and tradition. He had to stand alone within the community of His own disciples and challenge their lovelessness and shortsightedness when it became necessary. He did not expect to be loved or affirmed by everyone. The Son of man's clear sense of identity and self-governing autonomy carried him beyond the power of fear, through the cross/resurrection experience.

Paradoxically, He who was excluded from earthly privileges for Himself reassured His disciples: "Let not your hearts be troubled; believe in God, believe also in me. . . . I go to prepare a place for you" (John 14:1-3). Further, He pledged to return someday and receive them "that where I am you may be also." The inner meaning of *home* would be His presence with them. When one of His friends asked how He would manifest Himself to them, Jesus replied: "If a man loves me, he will keep my word, and my Father will love him, and we will come to him and make our home with him" (John 14:23). Jesus assured His followers of a place—a home for the heart—here and now, not just hereafter. Loving obedience would be the basic qualification for at-homeness with the Father.

People Without a Place

Now, let us transpose these understandings of *place* into local church and mission settings. When pastors move to a new congregation or missionaries relocate, how much help from their constituents shall they expect? Perhaps we can emphasize their feelings of placelessness by contrasting the pastorate with the presidency of the United States.

In the spring of Ronald Reagan's fourth year as US president, he visited the People's Republic of China. The announced purpose of the week's journey was to underscore the military-commercial significance of the "Asian Basin" for America's future. An entourage of negotiators had preceded Mr. and Mrs. Reagan to Beijing to formalize agreements with the Communist regime that would be signed in highly publicized meetings between the two nations' leaders. They were accompanied to China by more than 900 Americans, including Secret Service men and 300 news media personnel.[1] The Reagan party was headquartered at the $65 million Great Wall Hotel, a joint-venture luxury hostelry in Beijing's outskirts. No expense was spared in taking precautions and making all the right impressions. The president's own bulletproof limousine was used in China where the average per capita annual income is less than $250 (US). Conservative estimates of the tour's costs for government principals and their attendants exceeded two million dollars.

By way of contrast, recall from the previous chapter the picture of Dr. and Mrs. Wilbur Lewis, en route to their Paraguayan destiny, with their children and crated possessions on a tiny riverboat. Because of a mix-up, no one met them when they arrived "at home" in a strange land of new language, odd odors, different customs, and unique people. They and their worldly goods were set off a barge on a mud bank.

I recall a young pastor and his wife who had been persuaded by a church's search committee to help the people build a house for their minister family's use. Literally, there was no pastor's home or parsonage. It had been a part-time, student assignment filled by seminarians, as was the case in this instance. Because the young man had had a business background prior to entering a religious vocation, he was optimistic about the assignment. Cotton crops were good that fall. A builder in the congregation offered to construct a modest cottage at his cost, donating his own services as supervisor. Volunteer craftsmen helped with the construction.

During the months of planning, financing, and building the parsonage, a mild misunderstanding arose. Personalities were involved. Smoldering conflicts with the contractor's family that went back a quarter century surfaced. The idealistic pastor and his young wife, both from another part of the country, were caught by surprise in congregational cross fire. In supporting the builder, he inadvertently alienated certain ambitious laymen of the church. The student couple, though deeply dismayed, helped to complete the construction, paint, and decorate the interior (including curtains the wife made). But in the process they knew they were not "at home" in that place and determined to resign without occupying the house themselves. They left the congregation free of debt, yet they felt confused and hurt by the conflict's effect on their future and on the congregation's fellowship. The student pastor's idealism was permanently tempered by the conflict's abrasiveness; yet, he learned to be more patient and steadfast in dealing with human limitations.

Contrast that episode with another minister couple's experience in a metropolitan church setting. Moving in springtime, church officials and neighbors helped the pair locate and refurbish a suitable house, clean unwanted ivy from its exterior walls, sod barren spots in the lawn, and fix shelving for tools, storage, and sports equipment in the garage. Their occupancy of the house during Holy Week got off to a good start amid many calls from well-wishers, bringers of food and gifts, errand runners, and practical helpers. Their new congregation cared in deeds, not mere words. Having moved from another part of the country where folks were reserved and cautious, they were amazed by everyone's hospitality and friendliness.

I think of so many ministers and missionaries who have had to settle for modest provisions and transitory places in the world. The late Gordon Clinard once preached a sermon titled: "On Planting Trees We Never Sit Under." He knew about disappointment. Here are typical transient servants of God I've known:

- A missionary couple assigned to Vietnam who lost all their earthly possessions in wartime and barely escaped from the country with their lives;
- A pastor couple with a young child who lived in a makeshift, poorly furnished apartment in the church building itself;
- A middle-aged pastor ground down by years of hard work and training staff members who moved on to larger churches, but who himself was continually overlooked in his search for a more significant place;
- A home missions couple rejected by residents of an Indian reservation;
- A missionary couple driven by political conflict from their adopted country returned to the Mission Board's home office; yet, feeling displaced in the US, they sought reappointment overseas;
- A quadriplegic seminarian, injured in an overseas automobile accident, married a caring companion in hopes of being together in some sort of ministry. Yet there was no guarantee of any future place for them.

We have been thinking of people without a guaranteed place in religious vocations. How can persons charged with securing new pastoral leadership help to provide them security and a home for the heart?[2]

Opening the Door to a New Place

Churches with a congregational form of self-government employ ministry personnel through a search committee representing the entire fellowship. Here, suggestions are offered for selecting a new pastor who will feel compatible ("at home") with a particular congregation. The thrust of this discussion is on fitness or suitability for each other rather than methods of finding a pastor per se. Similar ideas might apply to any member of the staff leadership team. Guidelines are available from denominational offices and booksellers for search committee organization, agenda building, and prospect screening.[3] Churches with a hierarchical or delegated form of governance may receive assistance from the regional judicatory office like district superintendent, presbytery executive, bishop, or the like.[4] Unsolicited assistance often appears in the form of recommendations, letters, and calls from friends of ministers seeking a place of service, members of the congregation itself, seminary placement groups, and offices of denominational executives.

Screening for a potential pastor occurs at numerous levels over the course of the years: gaining church recommendations for a candidate's entrance to theological school, passing examinations and qualifying for graduation from an accredited seminary or divinity school, filling part-time positions in summer service, completing supervised clinical pastoral education, and satisfying an ordaining council of one's theological persuasion and professional competence in ministry. At bottom, however, the candidate must "screen" himself or herself by pursuing God's call in choosing a ministry vocation. No church committee can measure God's will in appointing a man or woman as Christian servant by His Spirit. Yet the Bible suggests, "Do not believe every spirit, but test the spirits to see whether they are of God; for many false prophets have gone out into the world" (1 John 4:1). One obviously "of the world" is not to be recognized as a spiritual spokesperson for God. Thus, the community of faith is to verify God's call.

Given this lifelong process of preparation for ministry, a search committee presupposes prior steps of winnowing in career clarification. The dual nature of its work is to represent a congregation fairly and faithfully to a prospective pastor and, in turn, to present the best qualified person possible for confirmation by the congregation. The focus here answers the question: "Whom do we desire as pastor in light of who we, the congregation, are?"

The search committee's composition should represent honestly the congregation's rich diversity. It will organize itself for its assignment, educate committee members for quality service, and agree on an agenda of work. Criteria for the new pastor, in light of stated congregational needs, should be determined and consensus reached before any contacts are made.[5] Each committee member will face upward for divine leadership, inward for church needs, and outward for a prime pastor candidate.

Search committee members may be certain that a prospective pastor will have his own priorities during their discussions. Experience has cautioned him to "look before he leaps." Further, he may not wish to leave a present place of effective service. Moves are not automatic—push/pull, click/click—affairs. Uprooting a minister's family is a major undertaking. Children may be in school. A spouse may have a career of her own. The prospective pastor's agenda may reflect a preference for another part of the country, challenge for gifts now dormant (like evangelism), family needs, provision for continuing education, desire for a larger staff, or need for increased total compensation.

Choosing the right pastor is more than a game of chance. It is a mix of art, prayer, skillful assessment, and faith venture in introducing pastor and church. No amount of sophistication removes the committee's obligation to follow God's guidance in their analysis and selection process. To facilitate church/ pastor fitness for each other, committee members should inform themselves by answering questions like the following.

1. *What is the purpose of our church and its ministry?* Here, a careful study of the church's past history is indicated. Prepare and provide committee members with charts of growth/decline in all areas of work as reported annually to denominational headquarters. Make facts accessible for a ten-year profile: resident members, new members, educational organizations, mission outreach, property value, personnel additions or changes, and finances. Picture clearly what the church's goals, growth patterns, financial investments, and accomplishments have been.

Given its constituency and staff, its building and budget resources, its denominational reputation and community feeling, growth directions and potential profile—where is our church headed in the next decade? Are there limited options because of circumstances like: changing neighborhood, membership depletion, no space for expansion, oppressive debt, hodgepodged programs, legal restrictions, or basic resistance to change? A potential pastor will align his gifts, interests, and life directions alongside the church's reason for being. He will ask himself: "Are our basic purposes parallel or in conflict?" A creative blend of purpose and potential is desirable for pastor and people.

2. *What does a life cycle analysis reveal about the constituency?* Some congregations move up the age scale imperceptibly, aging along with a minister, and become weighted with middle-aged and senior adult members. Other churches attract young marrieds or young executive families, singles, formerly marrieds, ethnic populations, college, or university students. Answering the question of "Who are we now?" charts the membership's age spread, targets under or overpopulated groups, and points toward growth needs.

Education and social class distinctions can also be spotted. For example, a church that has sponsored several new missions may have lost crucial leadership in the college educated, young adult sector. The search committee must spell out population statistics and growth potential before interviewing a key pastor candidate. In fact, its discoveries will help determine the age range, educational level, and professional experience desired in potential candidates. Many churches are more interested in the *kind* of minister desired than in an age range as they form a profile.

3. *How innovative and creative are our ministry programs? How open are we to change and modification of ministries?* There are three parties in the church-pastor match: the people and their mission, pastor and his potential, and Holy Spirit as matchmaker. Any move the congregation makes toward an exciting, open future will likely prompt a positive countermove from a prospective pastor. A search committee should be honest with its findings about the fundamental orientation of the church. Ostensibly, they are working for the congregation. But, in fairness, they are to whet the prospective candidate's appetite within realistic limits. Only an eager beginner will be fooled by the committee's overselling a church's assets and overlooking deficiencies. Better to level with each other during the interview process than to terminate a ministry early because of disillusionment.

For example, the former pastor may have worked a decade pointing the congregation toward relocation of the church plant. If he left discouraged because of passive or massive resistance, share impressions for a potential turnaround or continued conservatism with the candidate. Help him to assess potential obstacles and options for change.

4. *What does our balance sheet say about financial resources and liabilities?* A few congregations have income from capital investments and endowment funds to supplement weekly tithes and offerings. Such groups are real but also rare. Most church budgets follow the personal financial fortunes of their clientele. For

example, a disastrous fire in a major plywood manufacturing plant put some 375 blue-collar employees temporarily out of work. Assuming they were active church members, budgets would be over-spent for many months until the owners rebuilt the burned-out plant, and employees returned to work.

A prospective pastor discovered, in conversation with church leaders, that the congregation owed about $1,050,000 for a recent remodeling project. A friend suggested that he inventory the number of households in the church family who actually shared in the debt retirement process. Upon analysis, slightly over three hundred family or single units were determined to owe an average of $3,500 each. Assuming a ten-year loan with prepayment option, the debt computed about $350 plus interest per household per year—a manageable sum.

Are there anticipated expenses that cannot be changed? Will revenues increase, decline, or remain at about the present level in years ahead? Should a shortfall occur in receipts, what options have we to continue or cut programs and mission support? Are present staff salaries adequate, fair, and comparable with other churches our size? Answers to such questions will help determine the pastor's total compensation, the issue of a housing allowance versus provision of a church-owned parsonage, health and annuity, Social Security, as well as overall staff salary support.

5. *What is the prevailing mood or spiritual temperature of our people?* Some congregations have become burned out with workaholism, promotion from the pulpit, extractive financial schemes, endless expansion, and continuous change. *When is enough enough?* people wonder. Their favorite hymn becomes: "O land of rest, for Thee I sigh," and their determination is to move out of the fast track once the present pastor resigns. Some folks leave before he does!

Other churches have resigned themselves to a passive pastor whose laissez-faire administrative style leaves matters at loose ends or unraveled at the center. He may have neglected evangelism, discipleship training, and missions. The congregation may have loved him and remained loyal to him. Now, are they stuck in slow motion, or do they crave a more assertive leadership style?

Most church members live somewhere between the big push and passivity, residing somewhere on the "activity scale" between one and ten. You might ask, where are our people today: united or divided in purpose and program; liberal or conservative in theology and ethics; generous or tightfisted in finances; up or down in morale; positive or negative about the future; supportive or indifferent to present leadership; expectant or satisfied in outlook; up front or evasive about anger; and heroic or defeated in spirit? The prospective pastor will also be concerned with the church's cooperative attitude toward the denomination—state and national convention leaders. Does the church have a reputation of friendly cooperation or a stubborn independent streak? Have there been serious problems in the fellowship: with glossolalia, sexual aberrations, interpersonal conflict, or doctrinal divergencies? Likely, the search committee will find that the congregation is a collection of groups rather than of individuals. They are obligated to picture the church's unity mid diversity and pluralism to candidates interviewed in the search process. A closely related issue then becomes:

6. *Do we want someone who thinks/feels/acts like us or someone different from ourselves as our pastor?* Here is a wealthy, aging congregation, for example, that thought it desired a youthful pietistic promoter as pastor. He came to them from a congregation of young adult couples who had let him lead, relying heavily on his administrative skill and spiritualized salesmanship. In the new (for him) place, executives, leaders, and professional persons did not line up at his command. The hard-driving pastor's new friends and majority of conservative constituents quickly solidified into opposing camps. Sensing that he was damaging

both the church and himself by trying to remake it in his image, the pastor resigned in short order.

Someone has said, contentment in the membership should be the first gift of a church to a new pastor. True, the people want a pastor and wife "like us," regardless of their spiritual condition and prevaling mood. They hope to avoid rocking the boat at all costs. Mysteriously, contentment and craving for change can walk hand in hand as people and prospective pastor meet and merge in ministry together. Certain minor changes may be anticipated, perhaps in office or sound equipment, in worship format, or visitation schedule. More profound changes, in personnel and basic policies for example, require prayerful consultation with leaders, group consideration, and consensus. Hopefully, caution will give way to mutual commitment in mission and ministry as the pastoral family enters a new place.

Between Two Worlds

Most ministers and missionaries experience a certain kinship with NASA astronauts—travelers in interplanetary space. It is not that their skilled professions are parallel in high technology and high risk alone. Rather, like modern travelers among the stars, persons in ministry careers live between two worlds—present and future. Choosing a vocation in ministry involves what one has called inadvertent homesickness. There is always longing for a *place*. The missionary family, for instance, wings its way off to some foreign land, leaving roots and relationships in some homeland. Their adopted country, people, currency, language, foodstuffs, and customs may be less than exotic. They have been asked to count the cost of further family separation—with one child in international school, perhaps another in boarding school several hundred miles away. Aging parents may risk one overseas visit with them between furloughs. Living in Third World nations requires separation from one's roots, farewells to family members back home, cultural adaptation to simple (more innovative) life-styles, and adjustments to amoebas unlimited.

Language school follows orientation for overseas living—double dislocation from one's prior "stability zones." Mission family displaces parental family connections for shared conversations, planning, work, worship, mealtimes, prayer, play, vacations, and occasional conflict. The new land challenges one's reliance on former social roles and supportive relationships. In the initial months of adjustment there is much stress. Life threats seem to lurk in hidden places—from new foods and marketing procedures, to household servants, to sticky-fingered thieves that come with the territory. Child rearing more and more must adjust to the absence of one or both parents from the home. Two fully equal partners—both of whom are committed and commissioned to mission service—find old worlds fading, and new worlds emerging. Their new situation is ripe for spiritual growth or shattered relationships.

What about the pastorate in a revolutionary time? you wonder. Homesickness persists there, too. One couple had completed theological school; the husband had accepted a church assignment in a distant state—far from his childhood family. "We cried for hours as we drove north toward our new home," he later recalled. "Pulling up roots and starting over was one of the hardest things we had attempted in our lives. Our whole support network had to change."

Given the mobility of modern society, families are increasingly isolated. The spouse who follows her minister husband from place to place usually gets cut off from her relatives. Her husband goes to work each day; she may live in a neighborhood almost as a stranger. Her small children may be her primary companions for most of the day, or, after they are in school, perhaps a neighbor or a few friends. The pastor's wife longs to get into the community where she can talk with persons on an adult level, face issues that interest her, and grow through challenge.

The pastor's wife shuttles between two worlds of home and church. Given her educational background and previous experiences of work, travel, and creative pursuit, a wife may become restless. She really should not be blamed for finding her role as a homemaker somewhat limiting. Like most American women, she wishes to grow and be engaged in meaningful and demanding activities for herself. Being satisfied as "Mrs. Preacher" belongs to an age forever gone. On the other hand, she has no desire to compete with her husband or give up her home and family. What shall she do?

In a Roper poll, nine out of ten women surveyed preferred marriage over all other alternative life-styles.[6] By implication, the Christian woman married to a minister or missionary wants the best of both worlds. She enjoys satisfactions of her role as a wife and mother; she has no wish to exchange that role for another. In addition, she wants her personhood challenged to its full potential.

For this reason, women whose husbands are in ministry vocations are turning increasingly to activities outside their homes. Some of them enjoy church-related activities like: Bible study and prayer groups, mission-centered projects to reach and help persons with identified needs, arts and crafts, even competitive athletics. Others prefer community charity and social projects though they may feel such activities fail to provide them with a sense of true purpose. Some spouses have found satisfactions from cultural or creative pursuits: music, painting, book reviews, travel clubs, and stimulating social contacts. Many ministry spouses have entered the labor market. Money may be part of their motivation, but a quest for meaning may be more significant to them. Part-time career activities offer a solution for the both/and of many such spouses.

Jim, a pastor in his mid-thirties said, "I don't know whether I'm experiencing a middle-age crisis or what. I've been in my current pastorate two and a half years, but I'm experiencing some restlessness." Then wistfully, "I'm challenged with opportunities Grace Church is giving me, . . . still, I want to be all that I can be. Somehow, I would like the next move to be *the* place—a place where Jane and the boys and I could be for ten or fifteen years. Can you understand what I am feeling?" he probed.

"Yes," I replied, "I hear you saying you're homesick in your present home—that you are struggling to find a home for your heart."

Having gone to school in different parts of the United States and ministered in areas as diverse as the east and west coasts, Jim was still between a present and future world. A personal and professional growth career evaluation procedure was planned to help him and his wife in their joint search for the best place to be.

"In a secular vocation I could step up and ask for a new, more challenging position," Jim spoke softly. "But in religious vocation I feel like a girl waiting to be asked out on a date. This whole thing of God's will is rather confusing. Perhaps we shouldn't saddle Him with our own desires for maximum usefulness." I reassured him that his questing spirit was normal for this season of his life.

Jim and I agreed to talk again in a couple of months following his career assessment process. I assured him, meanwhile, that his restlessness was likely "mid-thirties itch" rather than a full-blown mid-life crisis. He agreed.

In a later chapter specific suggestions will be offered for covenanting with your new pastor to serve God together. Ideas will be supplied for getting off to a good start and supporting your minister's family. The focus here has been to help church members appreciate the professional caregiver's longing for a home of his own.

The Best Place to Be

Thoughtful persons will acknowledge that the modern world is populated with exiles and wanderers, refugees and displaced persons, migrants and émigrés. They jam air terminals in places with strange sounding names like Beirut, Bujumbura, Kampala, and Lusaka. They are the "Boat People" of Southeast Asia, Jewish immigrants settling the West Bank in Israel, employees of multinational corporations assigned overseas, and the military on duty around the world. They are mission volunteers seeking reentry to home settings after living and serving overseas.

Once a missionary single or couple casts off restraints of their American home and adopts a new land and people, they become prime candidates for reverse culture shock. This phenomenon occurs when one has identified so strongly with an overseas setting and population that he or she "can't go home again" to the United States. A couple discovered their "Catch-22" predicament through homesickness for Virginia while in Africa and profound nostalgia for Uganda while on leave in America. They had intended to resign and resume life in the States but returned to their field—home in Africa. Church leaders must be sensitive to such tornness of spirit.

How can you care for people in a world on the move? Like Barnabas in the New Testament, be an encourager. Pray for the caregivers. Befriend your new pastor and his family when they move into your community. Help them move in and get settled. Ask practically how you can help. Encourage your children to get acquainted with the pastor's youngsters. Share social occasions together. Treat them like other human beings; they are real people. Learn the birthdays of the pastoral family and acknowledge them. Make their special anniversary days *special* with notes of remembrance and gifts of recognition and appreciation. In a word, welcome them into the family. "Rejoice with those who rejoice," and "weep with those who weep" (Rom. 12:15).

A denominational leader once drove with a pastor acquaintance to a meeting in the nation's capital.[7] The young minister had impressed his associates with his graceful, relaxed manner of life. He appeared "at home" in his own skin. The executive asked him about that, to which he replied: "Part of it is me. Part of it comes from a decision I made a couple of years ago that I could walk away from it all and still be OK." The church official processed his response. "He did not mean he did not care, was not available, or was never afraid." Rather, the pastor had gained an inner freedom and could act freely. Having discovered a home for the heart, he differentiated himself from the congregation. Free of its awesome, inexhaustibly demanding claims, he could be God's person. He had made his place and discovered home in his heart. His security may have arisen, in part, because of his denomination's efforts to support the life and work of persons in ministry-missions vocations. (See Appendix 3.)

Notes

1. *Fort Worth Star-Telegram,* Apr. 22, 1984, p. 12-A.
2. Both the Home and Foreign Mission Boards, SBC, have technical, lengthy procedures for receiving inquiries and applications from prospective candidates, screening prospects, pursuing candidates to appointment and commissioning, providing orientation, and transporting the individual/family and its belongings to the field of service. Because of the greater number and comparative simplicity of securing candidates in local church positions, the pastorate is used illustratively.
3. See Gerald M. Williamson, *Pastor Search Committee Primer* (Nashville: Broadman Press, 1981); and *Pastor Search Committee Planbook,* ibid., for step-by-step guidance in looking for a pastor. My remarks are confined to helping the new pastoral family feel "at home" in a new locale.
4. Lyle E. Schaller, *The Pastor and the People* (Nashville: Abingdon Press, 1973), pp. 9-79, guides pastor search committees that share responsibilities with regional judicatory offices.
5. For guidance, see Williamson, *Pastor Search Committee Planbook,* pp. 14-16; and Schaller, pp. 45-55.
6. Citied in Elizabeth Achtemeier, *The Committed Marriage* (Philadelphia: The Westminster Press, 1976), p. 61, whose thinking has influenced my own at this point.
7. John C. Harris, *Stress, Power and Ministry* (Washington, D.C.: The Alban Institue, 1977), pp. 93-94.

5 Challenge:
Facing Stress in an Alien Culture

Caring for persons in ministry vocations requires understanding their committed sense of calling, desire for self-esteem, idealistic expectations, and need for security. Characteristics of contemporary ministers and missionaries parallel each other closely in these basic areas. In exploring the subject of stress, however, we must analyze widely different pressures impinging upon missionaries who live and serve overseas and American-based ministers.

First, we should be clear about the meaning and usage of the word *stress.* The late Hans Selye, Austrian-born founding father of stress research, described stress as "the rate of wear and tear in the body." Selye held doctorates in philosophy and science along with medicine. Thus, he was something of a philosopher of life as well as a careful observer of stress reaction. He discovered that generalized adaptive responses to stressors take place within the human body and mobilize the body's defenses to protect it against possible damage. He called these nonspecific reactions *stress.* Selye helped us to understand that stress is not always a negative thing. When an individual has resources available to meet the challenges life brings, one experiences a healthy level of stress. Unrelieved stress, however, may produce distress.

Some stressors in overseas living appear to be *situational,* unique to a given context. Christian missionaries and nationals who had lived in Rhodesia, under the government of Ian

Smith, for example, faced radical changes when his British-oriented regime collapsed. An African leader with strong socialist leanings set up new rules and policed certain people closely. English identification was systematically obliterated. The country was renamed Zimbabwe for a famed archaeological site in northeastern Southern Rhodesia. Cities were redesignated with African names; Salisbury, the capital, became Harare, for example. Missionaries in the country, as well as nationals studying overseas who returned home to work, discovered they had lost touch with their origins.

Consider some of the contextual changes that made "life as usual" impossible in Zimbabwe. Political and economic ties of that nonaligned Third World nation were turned toward Russian Marxism. Tribal violence and struggles for power became common. Ancestor worship and primitive cultic rites were reintroduced to public school children. The status of aliens had to be renegotiated periodically. Sources of foodstuffs, medications, manufactured goods, and petrol became unreliable. Violence flared so frequently that some residents feared for their safety and fled to other lands. Others, by their presence, could have jeopardized the welfare of nationals. Numerous missionaries, though not all, requested transfers into neighboring countries with fewer hassles, risks, inconveniences, and losses. Where finances and circumstances permitted, some nationals emigrated to other countries and continents.

Other stressors and responses overseas are highly *personal.* A missionary spouse is killed in a plane crash; the survivors elect to go home to America. Another spouse survives her husband's death from degenerative illness and elects to stay overseas. Missionary colleagues may differ deeply over mission philosophy and policy implementation. Certain Christian workers have been so consumed with hostility toward one another that resignation seemed their only "out"; others adapted to differences and stayed with assignments.

Because of such factors, missionaries are people seeking definition who must adjust to an unstable environment overseas. Here, we note certain sources of stress and distress. A bit later, we shall look at coping behavior and survival responses.

People Seeking Definition

Uncertainty is the situation—spirit of the times—of Christian missionary living. In many parts of the world, persons on mission are forced to live as aliens and sojourners "in a strange land" (Ex. 18:3, KJV).

I once visited with the young son of ex-missionaries to Cuba, a couple who had served under Home Mission Board appointment for a decade in theological education. "How would you describe events in your lives after Castro came to power," I inquired.

"Things got tougher," came his cryptic and truly accurate reply. Consider with me some of the ways in which life becomes more complicated, and thereby difficult, following missions appointment. I am thinking particularly of challenges career missionaries face in overseas settings.

Missionaries Face Challenges of Self-Identification as Outsiders

A Nigerian national daughter of an evangelical pastor wrote after reading one of my books. Following warm greetings and introduction of her family, she stated: "We are blacks. Are you whites?" Six words said it all! Or did it? Actually, people of Caucasian descent—European, North African, and southwest Asian ancestry—form a minority of the world's nearly five billion inhabitants. Living in lands of black- and brown-skinned citizens, white residents stand out because of contrasting physical features. Beneath the exterior differences, however, they are more like host country residents than at first appears humanly possible.

Self-identification is an ongoing process of human development, starting in infancy and continuing as long as one lives.

Pediatric medicine has taught us that infants undergo stages of emergence into their family contexts like: showing interest in parent figures and surroundings, developing loving attachments to caregivers, making an emotional impact on family members, and imitating the speech, habits, and life-style of parents and siblings. And that first year of identification with other human beings is only the beginning. A young child learns to walk, communicate in a mother tongue, adapt to nurture or neglect from powerful providers, consume adult foods, control bodily functions, and initiate behavior as a member of a social system.

Perhaps humankind's most fundamental distinctions are those of gender, not race. Universally, life adjustments unfold in a drama of maleness and femaleness, as well as of one's inherited traits, cultural values, and human potentials. Third World nations are generally cultures of poverty, inequality, competition, cruelty, creativity, and endurance. Through the years, a person adapts to sex role expectations in a unique environment. One learns a particular culture's lore and history, risks and rewards, ways of work and play, symbols and options, family routines, religious rituals, and group survival techniques.

Recalling one's own life history reminds us of how deeply etched are the markings of being a White Anglo-Saxon Protestant (or Catholic or Jewish) citizen of the United States. To become a missionary, a person must willingly become a foreigner and experience strangerhood in another country. Yes, become an ethnic in an alien culture. Ethnic is from the Greek *ethnos*—meaning a nation or people classed according to common traits and customs. If a person born in Switzerland or Swaziland, for example, moved to Kentucky to continue his or her education in medical school, one set of assumptions would prevail. One would be a temporary nonresident, student alien. However, were you to leave your stateside work, family of origin, and friends and move permanently to Taiwan or Peru or Uganda, self-definition would become more complicated.

Imagine yourself settling into a new land as a foreign born alien and facing living arrangements, language requirements, and government regulations affecting outsiders. The effect might be somewhat like learning to walk, talk, and perceive reality all over again. Go a step further. National Christians wonder about the intent, personality, and spirit of each missionary. Studies suggest the most significant "shock" potential in the strangerhood of extended overseas living experience is self-discovery.[1] Such new self-identification challenges previous conceptions of self and, by implication, the social world which sponsored them. One begins to see America through changed eyes! Given this self-discovery process, what might be required in socialization in a different culture?

Missionaries Face Challenges of Cultural Adaptation

The daughter of ex-missionaries had an opportunity to return for six weeks to the country where she had lived for eight years. While all the other volunteers in her group were seeing Southeast Asia for the first time, for Judy it was like going home again. Here are some of the adjustments she remembered having to make as an MK (missionary kid) when her medical doctor father took his family overseas.

First, there was a completely new language to learn and communication barriers to transcend. In some lands, MKs study at home, using curriculums like the Calvert system, with parents as teachers. The primary burden of establishing a teacher-student relationship, classroom surroundings, learning resources, and study disciplines falls into the mother's hands. Given less remote settings, journeyman missionaries often take a two-year teaching assignment with MKs overseas. In other cases, volunteer educators work with small groups of MKs, usually in an interdenominational setting. Still other youths attend national schools with local children, as though they

were citizens of that country. Some MKs attend international
school with children of diplomatic, business, and military personnel. Others must leave home and reside at a boarding
school, seeing parents only during vacations and holidays.

Seven-year-old Cindy, for example, found herself in a
French-speaking school in West Africa where her father served
as an evangelist rather than in English language classes in
Florida where she had lived before. Cindy may have been
pretty, white, and bright in America, but her sense of worth
plummeted toward zero in a black world. A lot of tutorial work
in French was required for each family member along with
extra effort in her basic course requirements. Social adjustments, including extensive absences when her father had to be
away from home, were angering and frustrating to a small girl.
Fortunately, a volunteer teacher took an interest in Cindy, gave
her personality and achievement tests, worked with her parents, and encouraged them to make adaptive changes together.

Let us return to Judy's cultural adjustments in Southeast
Asia. Beyond language and communication, new overseas residents must adapt to housing provisions made by their sponsoring organization. Some groups have well-established to quite
excellent living arrangements. In Third World nations, white
American missionaries appear well-to-do—with money, vehicles, and property—in contrast to most nationals whom they
seek to reach for the Savior. Some groups own, others rent,
places of residence for career and short-term staffers.

Certain missionaries prefer to "go native" in matters of
housing, servants, social customs, ceremonial forms, food, and
clothing attire. Urban living in an educational or medical center
is often in neighborhood style with other missionaries, though
not in the old compound fashion of nineteenth-century China
missions. A sponsoring agency might purchase property and
construct several houses or a cluster of apartments adjacent to
each other. Given various needs for transportation, communication, health care, and social support, cluster housing makes

sense. In certain parts of the world, property values have escalated, making it almost prohibitive to acquire permanent housing. In rural areas, missionaries can experience considerable isolation, loneliness, and dependence upon nationals.

Living arrangements prompt thoughts of further cultural adaptation like: adjusting to live-in servants in one's home, risking theft and using security devices, employing night watchmen, and keeping guard dogs. Years ago when I first began teaching in Third World settings, the barred windows and triple-locked entrances into missionary housing caught my attention. Break-ins are such common occurrences that residents of houses and members of churches must anticipate forceful entry of buildings. Newly arrived missionaries—outfitted with cameras, stereos, televisions, typewriters, sewing machines, and so on—provide easy targets for "hit" men. The foreigner's manner of life is carefully observed by local residents adept at living with limited resources.

Blending into the local culture requires acceptance of hospitality in the homes of nationals where cleanliness and sanitation may fall short of Western standards. Diet and food processing changes come quickly in rural areas where local residents depend upon gardens for fresh vegetables, orchards for fruit, local dairy farmers for milk (which has to be pasteurized), and wild game for meat. Poultry and fish are plentiful in most parts of the world though such meats can be quite expensive. Bread must be baked by the missionary homemaker or a servant; pastries and confections have to be prepared at home. City dwellers, on the other hand, have access to most products and food-stuffs to which we are accustomed in the United States.

As Judy revisited her former homeland, she recalled that health and medical resources were of uneven quality. The nearer to a metropolitan center one lives the better dental and medical care becomes. Surprisingly, good health care may be had in certain missionary hospitals, some of which have changed ownership and function under local government control. Missionary personnel with major surgical needs and serious health defects are often flown to American medical centers for care and to be near family or friends.

Missionaries Face Challenges of Emotional Ambiguity

Moving into a new land as an alien and adjusting to new ways of life, language, education, work, and worship frequently prompts mixed emotions for God's servants. For example, if one has been reared attending church services in a spacious Georgian or Gothic architectural-style building, one may at first shrink from primitive facilities in bush settings. The world's developed nations feature the finest architectural structures, but developing countries offer modest building resources. Meeting under a tree in an African or Latin American village with poles or split logs for seating is common. Dirt floors are quite customary. A metal roofed building may be considered a luxury. The only musical instrument may be a guitar or portable autoharp. "Going to church" means different things in different parts of the world.

While a missionary goes overseas with good intentions to win the world for God and love everyone, negative emotions may mount as frustrations grow. For example, Westerners are accustomed to living by stopwatch precision time, traveling and arriving at destinations on schedule, and beginning appointments at agreed upon hours. Have you ever heard of "African time" or "Latin American time"? Many Third World citizens wear no watch. They arise, work, eat, rest, and travel by sun and moon time. It is not defiance or discourtesy in their eyes to arrive late for an appointment or a worship service. When everyone finally gathers, they begin. Such a casual view of time galls some Westerners. "Wasting" time waiting for late arrivers sets nerves on edge. One's kindest thoughts may be clouded by what appears to be indifference or insolence. Really, it's the custom that prevails.

Newly arrived missionaries are struck by different relational patterns toward nationals developed in the past by mission family members. The ambiguity they face is captured in the question: "Shall we relate from a spirit of equality or paternalism with the nationals?" If one sees himself or herself as no-less-than and no-better-than a dark-skinned brother or sister, one relates in one mode of work and worship. Here, the view is: "We are equals in Christ" (Gal. 3:28). If, on the other hand, one relates downward from a paternalistic spirit of superiority, local citizens feel prejudice and respond with resentment. How much more effective one is relating as a brother or sister in Christ than as a powerful provider from the West!

There are many polarities of feelings as one settles into a new land and tries to serve God as a witness. One feels both love and fear—a desire to help others, yet wonder about what will happen next. Some Christian workers settle into place, develop creative ties with mission family members and nationals, and feel secure. Others keep up their guard, notice slights, experience homesickness, nurture resentment, and become frustrated. Emotions swing between desire to missionize, disciple, and congregationalize converts and dread of something going wrong. Such longing to reach nationals, yet fundamental dependence upon their acceptance, care, and responsiveness, is aggravated during wartime or periods of violent unrest.

You may wonder, for example, how missionaries can remain at their posts during a military coup d'etat like that in Liberia, West Africa, when President William Tolbert was brutally killed and his wife temporarily arrested. Or how can outsiders stay in Lebanon, torn so long by civil war?

One veteran missionary responded, "I've lived through so many coups, I can't afford to pay them any attention. I've been stopped by soldiers at roadblocks so often I no longer panic. I've learned to trust God and go on."

On the other hand, a missionary wife was so intimidated by the overthrow of a certain government that she retreated from relationships. After months of sleepless nights, fearful days, and depressed feelings, she took her children home to America. In time, her husband—torn between mission duty and family devotion—followed, resigning from overseas service.

Often, it is not just faith but flexibility that keeps a missionary functioning under fire. Conversely, brittleness or inflexibility may trap another caregiver in irreversible conflict. The competent missionary is not limited to the traditional options of "fight or flight" in stressful relationships. One can "go with the flow," adapt to minor irritants, change attitudes or even jobs, pray a lot, and survive. Unyieldingness and unforgiveness carry enormous price tags of bad faith, shabby relationships, and often poor health as well.

Missionaries Face Challenges of Vocational Clarification

New appointees overseas are often "on trial" among fellow missionaries during their first term of service. Some mission boards have a policy of prohibiting new missionaries from voting in business meetings for one year. While formally welcomed into the *family,* at a dynamic level a new couple or single feels closely watched in the beginning years. The gift of acceptance may become a prize which must be bartered for by pleasant behavior and ingratiating effort. Having to earn approval may result in denial of true feelings, blocked communication, and dampened enthusiasm.

The footnote here is that seasoned mission family members should be on their best behavior in receiving new appointees to the field. Love can be genuine and hospitality generous for newcomers—adjusting to climate, food, housing, language school, government regulations, and job expectations. Sharing an occasional meal helps soften the shock. Orientation for shopping, medical care, and local government protocol is essential. Getting children started in school requires assistance. While they do not expect to be "killed with kindness," beginners need clues to customs, supportive comradeship, and practical aid from veterans on the field. Local orientation can assist with such matters.

Missionaries are often thrust into jobs for which they are not well suited. New work assignments may be offered after arrival on the field. A church planter, for instance, may be asked to serve as a mission treasurer; a musician may be elected for one term as an administrator; or a dentist may be put in charge of an entire hospital. The spirit of service prevails among helping professionals; it's hard to say no when needs are everywhere. On the other hand, an evangelist may not be effective as a book store manager. He may know little about inventories, sales, and accounting procedures, let alone personnel policies.

There was, for example, a medical specialist, previously transferred from one country to another, who "made a stab" at operating a communications center. Without even trying, he succeeded in frustrating both nationals and fellow missionaries. Negativism, resentment, and criticism marred his ministry. In desperation, he was transferred to another country—his third job assignment in a relatively brief missions career.

Vocational clarification and accountability go hand in hand. Some missions operate with a policy that if a person fails at one task he is given another. One man reportedly changed "hats" over the years as a church development adviser, educational administrator, evangelist, and general repairman of missionary equipment (the job that earned him the most approval). Caring for such a caregiver calls for mid-career evaluation, gift assessment, and a carefully supervised assignment within the sponsoring group's guidelines. Incompetence, like laziness, is an ill-afforded luxury in mission service. For reasons like misassignment or maladaptation, some missionaries resign each year and enter different religious vocations.[2] Others adjust fortunately in an unstable world.

We have reflected upon stressors committed people experience while settling into overseas assignments. How can one know when one is facing too much stress, and what can be done about it?

Measurement of Stress

In the early 1950s, University of Washington psychiatrist Thomas Holmes observed that the single common denominator for stress is "the necessity of significant change in the life pattern of the individual." Holmes found that among tuberculosis patients, for example, the onset of the disease had generally followed a cluster of disruptive events: a death in the family, a new job, marriage. Stress did not cause the illness, Holmes emphasized—"It takes a germ"—but tension did seem to promote the disease process.

Holmes and psychologist Richard Rahe worked together in the 1940s and 1950s in an attempt to measure the impact of "life change events." They asked 5,000 people to rate the amount of social readjustment required for various events. The result is the widely used Holmes-Rahe scale.[3] At the top is death of a spouse (100 stress points), followed by divorce (73), marital separation (65), imprisonment (63), and death of a close family member (63). Not all stressful events are unpleasant. Marriage rates 50; pregnancy, 40; buying a house, 31; and Christmas, 12. Holmes showed that in a sample of 88 young doctors, those who totaled 300 or more units on the scale had a 70 percent chance of suffering ulcers, psychiatric disturbances, or other health problems within two years of the various crises.[4] Those who scored under 200 had only a 37 percent incidence of such infirmities.

Some authorities do not agree that major change events are primary stressors in our lives. They hold, rather, that everyday annoyances of life, or hassles, contribute more to illness and depression than major life changes.

In an effort to measure overseas missionaries' responses to stress, I have modified the Holmes-Rahe Social Readjustment Rating Scale. Of forty-two suggested "life change events," I adapted twenty-seven to a missionary's environment and left fifteen entries unchanged. The events are listed in descending order of probable stress point intensity. Fifteen mean values (stress points) were modified, and twenty-seven remained unchanged from their original scale. The inventory, provided here, was used to measure stress awareness among forty-four missionaries in one East African country. Limited research is available on the difficulties of missionary life.[5] My study was exploratory in nature with a focus on assessing the right issues and asking appropriate questions. Since the instrument was not normed on a large cross-sectional population, my interpretations of significance are tentative and viewed as directive for further study (see Figure 1).

A Note About Method

The Life Events were selected from suggestions during "listening sessions" with some 350 missionaries over a two-year period. Items were included which became recurring themes or concerns during the listening sessions in six nations of eastern and southern Africa, plus Israel and Gaza. Divorce was ranked second in the original and modified scales with an inflated mean value for missionaries. Usually, one's career ends if one's marriage ends in conservative church circles.

While longitudinal studies must verify my hunch, the gaining of a new family member (item 14) is so subjective and potentially stress laden that I introduced a sliding value from 39 to 70 stress points. Having an unwanted child differs from a happy pregnancy, for example. The birth of a Downs Syndrome or severely handicapped child suggests additional and prolonged family strain. Adopting or foster parenting a child overseas, particularly an unwanted or deformed child of another race, could be enormously stressful. Having a widowed parent or in-law move in with a family overseas, while only a temporary arrangement, might be like facing an earthquake.

Not all items apply uniformly to all mission situations. Item

Figure 1
Social Readjustment Rating Scale

Developed by T. H. Holmes and R. H. Rahe. Modified for professional persons in overseas assignments by C. W. Brister, Ph. D.

Rank	Life Event	Mean Value
1	Death of spouse, grief, adaptation	100
2	Divorce, life adjustment, and adaption	98
3	Moving into new culture, shock, and adaptation	80
4	Interpersonal conflict without resolution	75
5	Marital separation or death of close family member	63
6	Personal injury or illness (limited health resources)	60
7	Bureaucratic government restrictions	55
8	Fired from job (transferred from Mission at request of nationals or colleagues)	50
9	Philosophical differences in work (e.g., Mission Board vs. national initiatives)	45
10	Life transitions (e.g., missions volunteer, retirement)	45
11	Change in health of family member	44
12	Ethical failure of family member (e.g., son jailed)	40
13	Sex difficulties (e.g., unwanted pregnancy)	39
14	Gain of new family member	39—70
15	Readjustments in life (e.g., shortages of fuel/food)	39
16	Change in financial state (e.g., currency devaluation)	38
17	Death of close friend	37
18	Change to different line of work (e.g., if requested)	36
19	Suppression of human rights	35
20	Mortgage over $50,000 or major indebtedness	32
21	Siege mentality (e.g., blockade, travel restrictions)	30
22	Unreasonable demands by nationals (e.g., work changes)	30
23	Personal brittleness sets up conflict situations	30
24	Trouble with one's children or in-laws	29
25	Outstanding personal achievement	28
26	Furlough planning	26
27	Begin or end school	26
28	Change in living conditions (e.g., black marketeering, bribery, theft, beggars, servants at home)	25
29	Change of personal habits	24
30	Trouble with supervisor (e.g., work guidelines)	23
31	Inflexibility in deployment of personnel	21
32	Inadequate training of new personnel	20
33	Misassignment of volunteers/journeyman	20
34	Ineffective leadership from nationals (e.g., no vision)	20
35	Intransigence of Mission programs (e.g., new emphasis)	19
36	Too many jobs/failure to achieve satisfaction	18
37	Pulled between nationals (e.g., Arab-Israel)	18
38	Threat of war, attack	17
39	Betrayal of trust (e.g., disappointment w/nationals)	15
40	Accident, minor violation of law	15
41	Defining missionary role in eyes of nationals	12
42	Vacation, Christmas, holiday	10

21, "Siege mentality," occurs not just in war zones, but where nations' borders are closed, and travelers are hassled about currency, passports, work permits, and any goods in hand beyond personal effects. Subjective interpretations, including denial of reality and imagined resilience or toughness, kept some scores in the moderate range of my Kenya sample.

Discoveries and Observations

As we consider the scores which forty-four missionaries reflected, remember that psychiatrist T. H. Holmes established an illness predictor scale keyed to stress points. He and Rahe demonstrated there was a high risk potential of developing major illnesses within a two-year period after accumulating a certain number of stress points. Risk of illness is low if total points fall below 200, medium if points range from 200 to 300, and high if one's total points are above 300. If an individual collected as many as 300 or more points within a reasonably short time, he or she might develop a debilitating physical or emotional disorder within two years.

Eighteen persons in the Kenya sample scored under 200. Two items most frequently checked by this group were #15, "Readjustments in life" and #28, "Change in living conditions." A write-in item, "Chronic, periodic absenteeism of spouse" appeared on several instruments rated from 30 to 60 points. One respondent stated: "I am under more stress than the events noted indicated. Areas of stress for me are not necessarily listed."

Missionaries in the low-score group noted personal items that distressed them like: living with a spouse from a different background, temperament, gifts, and so forth; children's adjustments upon returning and living in the United States; local inefficiency, for example, telephones often don't work; language-culture barriers; family separation from parents and children; poor communication (time lag in receiving letters/

journals from USA); being white in a black world; limited language ability; and our wealth and their poverty.

Nineteen persons in the sample scored between 200 and 300, seven of whom were near 300 points with greater likelihood of illness. Again, missionaries facing more stressors checked the two items #15 and #28 a total of twenty-three times. Six respondents checked #26: "Furlough planning," a matter which preoccupies many overseas personnel. In certain instances, work efficiency is reduced for as much as one year prior to departure for the United States. Homesickness and anxious longing for restoration with people, places, and resources "back home" can turn a first termer into a liability on the field. One couple packed a crate of Africana months before furlough, took their young child and luggage to the nation's largest city some time before scheduled departure, and virtually abandoned their mission. Potentially, the privilege of leaving one's adopted country on furlough can create deficiency motivation and damage one's usefulness in cycles for a lifetime.

Fourteen persons, 32 percent of the total sample, experienced furlough planning as a major stressor. Such a stress index indicates that particular attention should be addressed to furlough concerns by mission board staff. A question frequently directed to my wife and me during overseas family enrichment conferences is: "What will happen to our children during furlough?" Behind that concern are fears of academic or personality deficiences developed imperceptibly during overseas residence and effects of peer pressure in the USA. The toughest stateside visit comes when the first child enters college and cannot return "home" overseas with the family. Veteran missionaries, conversely, appeared to maintain job efficiency closer to the date of their departure for the United States.

Five subjects, of forty-four sampled, scored from 308 to 400 points and landed in the high risk group for probable future illness. Two individuals scored over 400 stress points. Four of these seven persons checked item #4, "Interpersonal conflict without resolution" as a chronic stressor. Holmes and Rahe noted high scorers face a 70 percent chance of suffering physical or psychiatric disturbances within two years of the various crises.

In only one case was #1, "Death of spouse, grief, adaptation" noted. In the higher risk groups, some unique life events were added to the forty-two items listed: poor communication with sponsoring board (official communication channels do not function satisfactorily); relationships between the missionaries and local national convention leaders (Do they think we are doing an acceptable job?); absence of medical help, drugs, machine parts, all sorts of things; making decisions which affect lives of peers (heavy responsibility); fortress mentality because of possible break-ins; and inability to trust nationals to handle responsibility, keep promises, or pay debts.

The sensitivity of missionaries and concern for the common good may be observed in remarks like the following: stress to achieve the goals set in the shortest amount of time; using finances for the job in the most productive manner; seeing other missionaries suffer, and possibly go home permanently, without being able to help (or having tried, left it to the Lord). These concerns, along with absence from family in the US when they have crises, trying to befriend children 10,000 miles away, and uncertainties about a place and financial security during retirement years all add to the missionary's stress factor load.

Helping Missionaries Cope

The items noted above include primary areas of stress that overseas workers face in their daily lives. Laypersons back home, dedicated to "holding the ropes" and sharing partnership missions ventures, are learning more about the challenges of missionary life. They recognize that gaining foreign language fluency takes time, education of children is problematic, money may be scarce, family separation hurts, and privacy is a luxury for most mission families. Christian friends observe that many missionaries have learned to cope with stress. How may members of support groups in the United States assist with preventive maintenance?

First, let missionaries be real people—human beings who do not have to maintain a false image of strength. They live by faith and fortitude, just as you and I do. Why are God's servants expected to act in certain ways to uphold a "good image"? Some pastors and laypersons deny the reality of missionary humanness, remain insensitive when overwhelming stressors strike, and withhold help if one fails. (See ideas from the field, Appendix 4.)

Members of mission families also need to be real with one another. One missionary physician said: "Actually, if I had an emotional or spiritual problem there essentially would be no missionary to talk it over with. You can't be yourself." One must constantly scan the mission family and think of his or her behavior's effect on other missionaries. Having to be spiritually strong, wise, courageous, attentive to nationals' aspirations and needs, and morally flawless makes one vulnerable to loneliness, depression, and illness. Human beings need to acknowledge their limits.

Second, encourage missionaries in the wise management of anger. When persons are burdened, thwarted, or intimidated, one of the temptations they face is to become angry. Anger is not always a matter of choice, but the way in which we deal with it is.

Because their lives are stressful, "one may therefore expect that missionaries might respond with feelings of anger and frustration."[6] When they experience feelings of irritability, jealousy, negativism, suspicion, or hostility, some missionaries deny or repress them. The unexpressed anger remains unresolved. It may show up as passive-aggressive behavior in opposition to authority or indirect hostility toward a family member. Negative emotions left unresolved may lead to excessive guilt, physical illness, self-punishing behavior, or emotional breakdown.

The Bible suggests that anger in and of itself is not evil. Ephesians 4:26 tells us, "Be angry but do not sin; do not let the sun go down on your anger." There is much wisdom in working through ill will and resolving negative emotions. When the sun goes down on one's anger, surface reactions submerge into hostile responses that endure. What might have been handled properly as confrontation, clarification, or criticism may reappear as resentment, sarcasm, or hate. And unresolved hostility can lead to dreams of bitterness, verbal assaults, even open aggression. To keep an "enemy" in constant view or nurse old grudges against them is to alter one's body chemistry and run the risk of illness or unchristian behavior. It is much better to process differences as creative concerns, pointing toward resolution, than as occasions of wrath requiring condemnation or punitive action.

As a third resource for dealing with stress, help missionaries lay aside the unrealistic expectation of immediate acceptance and success. Third World residents are making giant strides toward freedom from dependence on powerful providers from the West. Self-reliance and use of their own resources humanizes people in underdeveloped nations. Thus, missionaries who go overseas with a colonial mentality and an imported Christianity are doomed to disappointment. They must prepare to face new political realities in emerging nations. Success must be reinterpreted in biblical terms.

One mission couple was shocked at the frankness of a Costa Rican student during an informal group discussion. "Who invited you to Costa Rica?" he asked heatedly one evening after their Spanish language classes. "Do you think you can fit Jesus Christ into our cultural patterns in Central or South America? How much of what you are teaching is Western culture, and how much is Christianity?" Exchanges like that were so heated in their early months overseas that the man became seriously depressed. His wife developed hepatitis which gave them an "out" to resign and return to a stateside ministry.

Fourth, national/missionary tensions can provide learning experiences which may eventuate in personal growth and Kingdom advancement. Rejection by nationals poses special problems for missionaries. Sometimes, new arrivals overseas are robbed or "ripped off." Such insults may not be personal but generalized toward Westerners. Rejection of one's overtures of aid—whether tangible, like food products or vegetable seeds, or intangible, like offers of love in the Savior's name—may come.

One native of Zimbabwe was quoted as saying, "I saw the emptiness of imported Christianity. It has not helped the people to establish their own identity. The colonial Jesus Christ was no good for the African. Missions failed to prepare the people for leadership—it was a master-servant relationship."[7]

Relational stresses remind us of our limits and invite us to new reliance upon God and one another. Stressors have a way of getting our attention. When opposition comes, health fails, or relationships shatter, new learning opportunities are at hand. Viewing such challenges as growth opportunities expands one's perception and generates genuine efforts toward understanding.

And that leads to a fifth resource for dealing with stress. Practice an intercessory prayer ministry for Christian missionary friends. The demands of their work often exceed their strength.[8] Birthdays are a reminder on a daily prayer calendar. The vague "God bless our missionaries around the world" is too impersonal and global. Prayer requests come in personal correspondence with mission friends. Lift them up regularly to the Father. Give attention to their specific concerns. The realization that people at home pray faithfully for them encourages God's servants overseas. Prayer is a powerful force in life, generating assurance of care—human and divine.

We have been reminded that stress is a universal experience in life. Stressors tell us that we are in "the same boat" with other ordinary people. We have had an opportunity to consider unique challenges in overseas ministry. Our perceptions have broadened, and our desires to help Christian caregivers have gained understanding. Helping will depend upon accrued wisdom and the power that comes from God. Careful research into matters like MK adjustments upon returning to America for education, and recommendations about reentry assistance for overseas personnel will provide stress management potentials in years ahead.[9]

Notes

1. Study by D. A. Meintel, "Strangers, Homecomers, and Ordinary Men," *Anthropological Quarterly* (vol. 46, 1973), pp. 47-58.

2. There were 143 resignations by Southern Baptist Foreign Mission Board appointees in 1982, the largest number in forty years. See S. Lindquist, "Twenty to 50% Fail to Make It—Why?" *Evangelical Missions Quarterly* (vol. 12, 1976), pp. 141-46.

3. T. H. Holmes and R. H. Rahe, "The Social Rating Scale," *Journal of Psychosomatic Research* (vol. 11, 1967), pp. 213-18.

4. "Stress: Can We Cope?" *Time,* June 6, 1983, pp. 56-66.

5. Considerable work has been done in the area of culture shock, which is peculiar to extended overseas living experience. A study by J. P. Spradley and M. Phillips, "Culture and Stress: A Quantitative Analysis," *American Anthropologist* (vol. 74, 1972), pp. 518-29, suggests there are universal stressors encountered by those who experience culture shock. These stressors include: inability to communicate satisfactorily, lack of social support, loneliness, and nonbelongingness.

6. Beth Corey Taylor and H. Newton Malony, "Preferred Means of Hostility Expression Among Missionaries: An Exploratory Study," *Journal of Psychology and Theology* (Fall 1983), Vol. 11, No. 3, p. 219.

7. "Missionary Cites Lack of Education in Africa," *Fort Worth Star-Telegram,* May 25, 1984, p. 19-A.

8. Intercessory prayer for missions is illustrated by Helen Jean Parks, *Holding the Ropes* (Nashville: Broadman Press, 1983).

9. See unpublished Ph.D. dissertation by Lynn Moss, University of Virginia: "A Comparison of the Children of Missionaries, International Students, and American Students on Measures of College Adjustment and Loneliness," 1985; and extensive bibliography by psychologist Clyde N. Austin, *Cross-Cultural Reentry: An Annotated Bibliography* (Abilene, Tex.: Abilene Christian University Press, 1983).

6 Finitude:
Coping with Human Limitations

Our purpose here is to picture the world as an ordinary Christian minister might experience it. This effort to comprehend ministerial vocation could be called "Operation Understanding." Thus, we will need to discuss lively issues, admit honest realities, and permit helpful facts to come to light. What is it like, for example, for a pastor to reconcile idealism with flesh and blood situations? What resources are available in a Christian worker's behalf, and how can one be encouraged to use them? How can you, a concerned individual, share the work of Christian ministry under the Holy Spirit's leading? Are there practical ways you can help your minister avoid problems and remain effective in obedience to God's call? Such concerns are in line with our theme of caring for professional caregivers.

I am thinking, too, of sensitive young persons who may be considering some vocation in ministry. Certain issues may be raised here that you would like to talk about with a trusted friend.

Ministers and missionaries must try to master the art of blending the spiritual and functional—the ideal and real in life. Southwestern Baptist Theological Seminary has a unique architectural feature. A domed stone building dominates the campus, located in a southern sector of Fort Worth, Texas. To the idealistic young student or occasional campus guest, the Memorial Building may appear initially like a surrealistic spaceship from a far off planet. Things look exciting—"out of this world"—a place of constant religious renewal. That fanciful image alters in time as one's workload increases, faculty expectations mount, financial stressors arise, and health limits appear.

To the diligent, initiated student or seasoned faculty veteran the dome on campus may appear more like the top of a pressure cooker than a spaceship. Getting into the ministry is rather like that. Initial illusions and fancies soon fall away. Profound spiritual strength and devotion to God, as well as physical stamina and loyalty to one's people, are required in the world as the Christian minister experiences it.

The World as the Christian Minister Experiences It

Most persons who have answered God's call to a vocation in ministry are positive in the face of recognized problems. More than just another job, they find church work challenging and exciting. It demands their best. Naturally, there are concerns like: having enough money to pay bills, counseling cases without easy resolution; negative mind-sets in the congregation; lack of privacy and continual interruptions of family time; power struggles with leaders; and what appears to be unfounded or unjust criticism.

Sexual improprieties are vocational suicide in the ministry. Such "exit" behavior sabotages effectiveness. Church members are charitable toward ineptness in the staff, even patient with some forms of presumption. But gross arrogance, demonstrated incompetence, and unethical behavior negate the gospel. Such serious symptoms call for radical therapies.

Most ministers find themselves functioning somewhere on the scale between "modest success" and "possible failure" in their day-by-day work. Let us put on the minister's hat briefly and perceive the world from his or her perspective.

A Voluntary Enterprise

A Christian minister looks at the church as a divine-human community. He understands Christ created the church, not we. "Christ loved the church and gave himself up for her," wrote the apostle Paul (Eph. 5:25). Those persons who receive the divine gift of salvation are baptized into a human institution. While their citizenship is in heaven and their calling is to advance God's kingdom, they live mid earthly limitations (Phil. 3:20). God's appointed ministers know the pain/joy of working with frail creatures of dust. They "have been very thoroughly initiated into the human lot with all its ups and downs" (Phil. 4:12, NEB).

In the very best sense possible, a local church is a voluntary organization. To use an athletic term, the average parishioner —no matter how well prepared in his or her own vocation—is a walk-on amateur at church rather than a highly trained professional. There are exceptions, of course. Unpaid workers may be depended upon to the degree of their giftedness and personal devotion to God and His work.

One pastor expressed his dependence on volunteers thus: "There are as many levels of commitment to the Lord and His church as there are members." The layperson can walk out on a church position as readily as he or she walks into it. Abandoning one's Sunday School class or a major committee assignment may be a matter of personal choice, crisis, or convenience, not criticism of paid staffers. Still, people who leave the church in a lurch can frustrate and disappoint the pastor and professional staff leaders.

A minister cannot put rigid attendance and performance demands on church members. He cannot require that they always be present. He cannot withhold spiritual blessings from persons who are halftime or quartertime attenders. Keeping an attendance record is not his job. Neither should he keep books on their financial contributions. A financial secretary usually has that assignment. Yet, he may well suspect that church attendance and giving records are clues to Christian character and commitment. Expressed positively, ministers feel they could be more effective in the Lord's work if they shared it with a team of committed people.

Pressure to Win

Americans divide the world into winners and losers. Children are taught to win, almost at any price, from their youth up. Churches are enmeshed in the merry-go-round culture of Wall Street, professional sports, politics, television make-believe, and multinational corporations. *Bigger* is the magic word. Worshiping at the shrine of Goddess Success, the unpardonable sin is to fail. The net effect is for ministers to compete— not only with the world but with other churches—and to become alienated from their fellow pastors.

"There has been that nagging gut feeling," noted a minister with over thirty years' experience, "to achieve, to be successful. No one likes to fail, and this is just as true for the Christian pastor." Somehow the minister is looked upon as a miracle-worker, a kind of superhuman Hercules who can perform endless labors imposed upon him by God and men. Health, patience, and strength must never fail. Endowed by some congregants with magical powers, he is viewed as one who can get unusual results with God. But what is it like to live within that mythos?

A veteran minister can tell us, "I feel that pressure on me— partly from the people I serve, partly from myself. We all want to see the church grow, numerically and spiritually, and because I am one of the leaders, I must make it grow." Being a good man or woman in ministry is essential but not enough. One must be good *at* growing the church and good *for* its institutional image. Looking at the situation objectively, a church staffer knows that no mere human grows God's church. Ultimately, it is the Lord Himself who blesses or withholds favor. Yet the sincere gospel servant feels that one should be doing more, or doing something differently, to attain the goal of success.

Denominational leaders may compound the problem when they feature primarily megachurch achievers in publicity and programs. An elite group of pacesetters in prestigious situations become models of ministry for thousands of gospel servants. A promising go-getter is sought by a pastor search committee bent on turning a church around toward success as a corporate venture. When will we recognize that one billed as "God's ball of fire" is a potential casualty of consuming ambition?

Perils of a performance-based ministry include more than a leader's potential ill health—dishonesty, manipulation, family neglect, disillusionment, and doing-in fellow Christians. The system works with vengeance. One idea is that a person begins in some small situation and continues to move up, with experience, to larger opportunities with tenure and power. Others play the number's game—each year's report shows significant advances over the last year's, and so on. Certain ministers have been known to delete low attendance Sundays in order to give the appearance of a better average. Others include dubious data in overall summaries. Gimmicks are used by some religious promoters in an effort to manipulate attendance and audience response.

The ordinary cleric or missionary asks in soul-searching moments: "What have I achieved and where am I heading?"

As a layperson who wants the best for his church and staff, remember that our Lord never played a numbers game. He worked redemptively from honest motives in serving God (John 9:4). Jesus' joy was doing the will of His Father (John 5:30). Support persons in ministry who seek to serve in a Christlike manner. Remember that our efforts are part of a larger process where some laborers plant, others water, and still others reap the harvest (1 Cor. 3:4-9). The ministry, ideally, is a collaborative enterprise, but loneliness is sometimes over-powering.

Loneliness Is Real

Perhaps you know a pastor like a friend of mine who preaches about love and fellowship but appears to be one of the loneliest persons on earth. Set into a breed apart by divine call and ordination, a minister occasionally feels different—like a third sex in creation. Challenged to live as a human being among real people, the temptation is to play safe, remain aloof, and deny a fully human existence. Ministers are traditionally cautioned about having special relationships or close friends in the congregation. They are expected to speak out on sensitive, often controversial, issues. Some clerics and their spouses have been hurt by betrayal of their trust. Others who have made themselves vulnerable to stories from counselees or confidants have felt they must keep secrets locked in their minds and hearts. There is no one else with whom to share it, save a wise spouse or with God in prayer.

What is the remedy for this shut-upness into one's own self—a life unfreely revealed? A crisis of personal illness can rip open the cleric's robes of privacy. I have a minister friend who experiences narcolepsy as a lingering symptom of a partially removed malignant brain tumor. A private man has "gone public" out of the sorrow of his soul and the terror of his family's experience. He has told his story in open testimony. Other persons were telling it secondhandedly. Sharing has not been for Victor Brandt a "show-and-tell" affair. Rather, along with continuous medication, the shared burden makes each day's drag more bearable.

A pastor facing heart-valve replacement surgery in Houston's Texas Medical Center was cheered by the presence of laypersons from his church. Being in the competent hands of a noted surgeon helped. But his parishioners symbolized the caring hands of the Great Physician whom he had faithfully represented to them through the years. The white walls of the hospital surgical suite were not so chilling because of the warmth of their shared love.

Why wait for tragedy to face the truth of one's need for understanding and companionship? Confessional preaching allows laypersons to see beyond the shining image to "the shadow side" of reality. "Things that have happened to us have great potency when we allow them to happen through us in open sharing," noted one minister.[1] Confessional preaching is not emotional undressing before an audience but a way of sharing one's incompleteness, imperfection, and search for spiritual strength.

Family relaxation, vacations, fellowship with other ministers, continuing education events, and convention trips provide opportunities to relieve pressure and transcend loneliness. An understanding spouse or staff friend can share burdens and provide essential love and support. Laypersons may become befrienders of ministers through social and recreation events, sensitive listening, wise counsel, real presence, respect for confidentiality, and faithful prayer.

One may take heart in recalling that Old Testament prophets like Elijah and Jeremiah lacked community (1 Kings 19:1-10; Jer. 12:1-6). One can identify with Jesus Christ who, in the company of His own disciples, experienced loneliness (Matt. 26:36-46). Solitude, correctly used, can become a time for spiritual transformation.

Authority Is Tested

Psychiatrist Louis McBurney and his wife, Melissa, devote their lives to strengthening clergy marriages and fortifying persons for their ministries. After years of leading therapy groups at a retreat center in Marble, Colorado, McBurney observed, "At the core of many problems faced by clergymen are unresolved conflicts over authority and dependency."[2] What did he mean? You may recall that in chapter 2 we spoke of the universal need for blessing in one's family heritage. Parental figures have authority over and obligation to bless their dependent offspring. I am using *authority* here in the basic sense of employing "power to influence or command thought, opinion, or behavior."[3] As a person matures, one learns to exercise authority in interdependent relationships. The blessed minister depends healthily upon God and his people and, at the same time, exercises appropriate authority in leadership. How is this authority earned?

Ancient monarchies were guided by a precedent called "the divine right of kings." One gained authority by birth and a blood line. Eldest sons acceded to the throne at the death of their fathers. They did not have to be expert or wise in order to rule; their position itself commanded followship.

Christian ministers do not lead in the historic sense of divine right. While proceeding under holy orders to serve God, a modern pastor must earn the right to lead. A congregation authorizes one to minister by its call, confidence in his gifts and preparation, and concentration of power in the leader's hands. Despite temptations in that direction, such empowerment is not blind. The responsible congregation insists properly upon staff accountability. Staff members are stewards of freedom and power in behalf of the church.

An authentic leader has his authority/dependency needs sorted out. An overly dependent minister is more of a puppet than a prophet. Someone else must motivate his work, guide his steps, supply ideas, monitor decisions, and approve behavior. Often, this is a powerful layman or clique in the congregation. An opposite temptation is for the minister to become a dictator—preempting the congregation the privilege of decision making and shared ministry. This misuse of pastoral authority—experienced by laypersons as bullheadedness, stubbornness, or strong-willedness—springs from *insecurity* or *presumption* but not caring leadership. Democratic authority lies between these two extremes.

Despite the purity of one's motives as minister or mission-ary, one's work may be called into question. The mind-set of certain laypersons leads them to oppose pastoral authority. Education may intimidate them; white collars may bother them. One pastor noted that certain personality types tangled in power struggles with him. "They come across as unable to trust their spiritual leader with the work they have called him to do." Working in the midst of opposition proves a frustrating experience at many points. "We become preoccupied with the rightness of our position, or the wrongness of the other per-son's view."4 Later in the chapter we shall examine a typical procedure for resolving such conflict.

Healthy Christian leaders depend ultimately upon God for assignment of a place to serve, acceptance of their gifts, guid-ance in the work, and blessing or approval of ministry. Their hearts must be right before the great King of creation (Ps. 1:1-6). By faith, they walk the path of righteousness which God appoints that it may shine "brighter and brighter until full day" (Prov. 4:18). While subject to challenge and criticism, their work is not as men-pleasers but as "servants of Christ" (Eph. 6:6-7). In such assurance, one's authority may be tested, practiced, and demonstrated as authentically from God.

Integrity on the Line

The authentic minister must be a person of impeccable in-tegrity. Life has a way of testing "the spirits to see whether they are of God," exposing impostors, and indicting religious pretenders (1 John 4:1). To reflect on integrity is to consider the need for wholeness and holiness—mental health as well as moral uprightness. Ministers and missionaries are capable of sinning and liable to sin. Like other Christians, they are never done with the need for forgiveness and growth. Thus, we are compelled to consider certain aspects of integrity in ministry.

One, a Christian minister must be a believable person—someone others can approach in absolute confidence. That is the ideal, not flawlessness but trustworthiness in basic character. Perhaps you have seen or shared a conspiracy of pastor/staff/people who want perfection in leadership. Such a goal is doomed to the emptiness of wrong expectations. Yes, religious workers are to mirror the "mind" of Christ Jesus and take "the form of a servant" in daily obedience to the Father (Phil. 2:5-7). All Christians, in fact, must "press on toward the goal for the prize of the upward call of God in Christ Jesus" (Phil. 3:14). But we fall short of total perfection on earth.

Laypersons must not give up on ministers and missionaries who are clay footed. The gospel treasure they bear is in "earthen vessels," and it is "by the grace of God" that they are what they are (2 Cor. 4:7; 1 Cor. 15:10). They are irrevocably human creatures but must not choose deliberately to become wolves "in sheep's clothing" (Matt. 7:15) or forsake God's flock (John 10:12). The character disordered minister who is fundamentally dishonest concerning money, sex, time, or truth—irreverent toward God and human personality—cannot endure in Christian calling.

Two, a minister should exemplify biblical wisdom and Christian vision. God's person lives by the Old Testament promise: "My [child], keep sound wisdom and discretion; let them not escape from your sight, and they will be life for your soul" (Prov. 3:21-22). One does not pursue wisdom for wisdom's sake, but for the Kingdom's sake, church's sake, and one's own individual or family's sake. Let us consider sample needs for clear-eyed wisdom and vision.

The pastor is frequently placed in the role of mediator in personal, institutional, and community affairs. Members of his own or church family may become conflicted with one another or within the congregation or public school system. He is inadvertently drawn into the conflict as presider and peacemaker. Various needs of the church staff and of one's people become opportunities for ministry. Pastoral friends on both sides of an issue may become involved in some difference or difficulty, then dump the problem into the pastor's lap. The issue may be as simple as guidelines concerning use of the church nursery facilities or as complex as divorce proceedings. A difference may arise between a staffer responsible for use of the church van and workers requesting it. Far more complex are differences of conviction concerning the church's basic mission, patterns of ministry, denominational relations, personnel issues, use of money, and construction of buildings.

Christian leaders symbolize the "gift of tomorrow" in their places of service. They must be farsighted visionaries, tuned to the Holy Spirit's impact, and capable of holistic wisdom. They both compete with and make use of media to gain peoples' attention. As a secular saint, the preacher must know both the world and the gospel. He is expected to be faithful to global needs—like peace, earth care, and world hunger—yet be able to gaze through the private window of one human heart and meet personal needs, too.

Tempted toward activism and accomplishment, the spiritual guide must be given to introspection and observation. Hear one minister's confession: "So intent have I been on promoting my own ideas, agendas, plans, and projecting them on other people and situations, that I have not been patient, still enough inside, humble enough before other realities . . . just to observe what was there."[5] C. S. Lewis once wrote a fascinating book about powers of observation— *Til We Have Faces.* Both men are calling us to observe people well in life, enjoy nature, and sense earth's minute textures and pleasures.

The world as the Christian minister experiences it is both "out of joint" and filled with promise. Just now, the issue is how you can help some minister friend cope with human limitations and, thereby, strengthen his effectiveness. There is a yearning for wholeness among "wounded healers," and some good things are happening.

Helpful Things Are Happening

Perhaps you've heard of the novice visitor in a modern hospital who sought to encourage a seriously ill friend. He intended to strengthen the heart patient who was breathing with difficulty under an oxygen mask. The ill friend was unresponsive as the would-be helper sought to engage him in conversation. The patient desperately struggled for air and whispered: "You're standing on the oxygen tube." Intending to enhance health, the guest inadvertently endangered his friend's life.

Some ministers, like Jacob of old, are wrestling with angels (or demons) and seeking a certain blessing from God. Laypersons may misperceive their struggle and, in effect, stand on the oxygen tube. They need comradely support to overcome isolation and the burdensomeness of a pretended superhumanity. This is a day of individual effort in numerous independent-type churches. Yet as Dostoevsky once wrote: "True security is to be found in social solidarity rather than in isolated individual effort" (*The Brothers Karamazov*). Are there signs of mutual concern?

More laypersons are becoming aware of and sensitive to clergy needs. They are encouraging pastors to plant their lives in particular places and stay beyond the two-year average tenure in numerous churches. They appreciate Lyle Schaller's wisdom, that *"from the congregation's perspective* the most effective years of a pastorate *rarely begin before* the fourth or fifth or sixth or seventh, and sometimes even the eighth, year of that pastorate."[6] Of course, there are exceptions to that generalization.

Missionaries are provided periodic furloughs and growth opportunities away from overseas assignments. More than 40 percent of Southern Baptist missionaries who resigned in one recent year had been on the field less than five years.[7] To help minister to such persons' needs, the Foreign Mission Board now requires on-the-field evaluations and conducts debriefing sessions for returning first termers at its Missionary Learning

Center near Richmond, Virginia. Encouragingly, a total of forty-eight former missionaries were reappointed to the mission force in one two-year period. The board has sought to improve communication with those who for a variety of reasons have had to resign and return to the United States.

How can laypersons aid professional caregivers in practical ways? Welcome pastoral and staff families warmly when they move to your community. Help them settle in with housing needs, child care, moving tasks, useful welcome gifts, and orientation to community and area resources. Learn wedding anniversary and birthday dates and celebrate such special occasions. The deacons in one church have joined in giving their pastor birthday gifts that have included sporting goods, clothing items, camera equipment, and a chain saw for firewood provision. Friendly hospitality, hosting meals at home or in restaurants, and assurance of friendship and prayer support are appreciated by minister families. They, in turn, reach out and care for members of the congregation.

Second, churches are building in growth opportunities for permanent staff members. Continuing theological studies are anticipated in the calendar and supported in the budget. Some staffers elect a periodic study session in their own or a different school than one of their initial preparation. Institutes and workshops in special areas—like media use, computerization, church growth, discipleship, preaching and worship planning —are being provided by major denominational groups. Pulpit exchanges and partnership missions encourage ministry opportunities in overseas settings, expand horizons, and challenge the minister's vision.

One way to encourage your pastor or staffer to stay is to build extensions of vacation periods at three-, four-, or five-year intervals. Insist that ministers facing constant pressures and numerous evening meetings take one or two days off each week. They merit family time and deserve a right to rest like other human beings. Sundays should not count as a rest day since, for them, it demands heavy expenditure of work time and energy. Body care is essential to avoid chronic fatigue or serious illness.

As a third resource, denominations are providing development opportunities for ministers' use which laypersons can encourage. Testing, career assessment, small group evaluation, and expert individual feedback are available through personal and professional growth seminars. Christian conference center programs and denominational resource persons are available electively to both ministers and laypersons. Telecommunications and media resources are being continuously developed and expanded for church program and personal growth use.

Counseling services and family enrichment opportunities available to ministers and missionaries are a fourth resource. You do not have to reflect long on the calls for help, sometimes unreasonable expectations, and interruptions ministers face to imagine family life unraveling at the center. Even the healthiest homes can produce some spouse and parent-child conflicts. Religious workers still at war with their own heritage, guilty over some attitude or act, or chronically angry at life run risks of depression and other disorders. Marital infidelities, prescription drug or alcohol abuse, and escapist behavior are symptoms of deep-seated clergy difficulties. But such behaviors also become problems in and of themselves.

Earlier, reference was made to the therapeutic retreat center guided by psychiatrist Louis McBurney in Marble, Colorado. It typifies the numerous counseling services now being provided for ministers and missionaries by private and church-oriented groups. Certain denominations contract with local pastoral or medical specialists for clergy family care.

There are individuals, of course, who protest against any notion of help for helpers. One pastor wrote a letter to the editor of a religious journal denying human limits. He closed thus: "I pray that instead of pastors and their wives seeking family enrichment systems or psychologists that they seek the

Lord and His will for them. I am not distrusting such activity, but I trust the Lord more. . . . He works better and quicker every time."[8] To which the editor replied wisely, "It is possible that the Lord can lead some ministers to recognize their personal problems and seek counseling from trained counselors."

That leads to a fifth resource laypersons will appreciate and encourage. Colleague sharing groups are getting together on a regular basis and helping one another come to grips with needs. John Claypool described such an experience while serving a Kentucky congregation as an event of "experiencing grace." A group of six clergymen from different denominations met uneasily at the call of a wounded minister who requested help. "When one lives as isolated from the depths of others as our competitive way of life demanded, one concludes that the shadows within oneself are abnormal—that no one else experiences such darkness."[9] Surprisingly, compassion was evoked, not rejection, as the veils were parted and helping professionals shared their common griefs. They discovered empathically that they were all grieving for the same things.

Our consideration of human limitations and helpful support provisions by persons, congregations, and denominational entities offers ground for encouragement. The implications are that pastors, chaplains, campus ministers, church staffers, and denominational specialists can't do everything by themselves. They need the shared wisdom, participation, conflict resolution ability, and prayerful support of church members and colleagues. Consider the potentials of a church-minister relations committee.

Church-Minister Relations Committee

Within the span of one week, five significant events concerning church-pastor relations came to my attention. Because they reflect traumas and trends in the larger fellowship of churches, I share them, plus a proposal, with you.

A pastor called to report that the ministry was not what he

had imagined it to be. "I may have missed my call," he said wistfully. "I seem to be drying up spiritually." His experience paralleled that of Roy Hobbs, the promising young baseball player, from Nebraska, in Bernard Malamud's novel *The Natural.* He dreamed as a boy of being the best athlete possible but, after a fifteen year mysterious absence from the sport, explained: "Life didn't turn out the way I wanted it to." The discouraged minister planned to seek employment with a denominational agency in which he could use his business background.

Another pastor returned from a well-deserved vacation and, surprisingly, received a visit from an outspoken deacon. The gist of their conversation was a reminder that most pastors had moved at the close of two years' ministry with that church. The deacon claimed to represent only himself, yet he suggested that since the pastor had completed two good years of ministry there, he and his family should move soon.

A layman confided that his pastor was working behind the scenes to dispose of the church-owned parsonage and to purchase his own house. He desired to accumulate an equity in property as part of a long-term savings program. He had failed, however, to bring the matter out in the open and discuss the merits of pastoral home ownership with his people.

A denominational employee related that his father—a seminary graduate and pastor of one church for the past twenty-one years—had resigned with no place to go. An intrastaff conflict, unresolved after a year and a half, had prompted his action for the sake of church unity and personal sanity. Sadly, there was no place for the mid-fifties father to go. He was thrust on the auction block again and "available" for supply/interim work or a new challenge.

The diaconate of a metropolitan congregation reacted negatively to serving several years as co-ministers alongside the staff. They had given up roles as administrators and become caregivers under the pastor's guidance but felt a loss of prestige in the people's eyes. After careful assessment, the deacons moved from a caring role to a more visible consultative role in all church affairs. With the resumption of control of administrative affairs, their family care and crisis ministry groups withered. Care for them was spelled *power* rather than service.

Personal dramas like these are typical of the growing pains, grievances, crises, complaints, and proposals for change occurring in churches throughout many denominations. And there are more: long-term, chronic illness for a staff person without disability insurance provision; a minister's sudden death and resultant family needs for housing and financial support; and major policy differences among staff members with no grievance committee to handle them. A hospital chaplain was involuntarily terminated when news of his divorce reached denominational headquarters. There was no board of appeal or review to consider his case. What can be done about such needs?

A pastoral relations committee for smaller churches and a staff relations committee for larger churches and denominational agencies could provide a suitable answer to such continuous dilemmas. Proposed initially by Lyle Schaller as a "survival tactic" for clergy, such a system could salvage missionaries and specialists in ministry also.[10] The group would meet periodically, perhaps every six months, with the pastor, chaplain, campus minister, or specialist in ministry. They would function as ombudsmen when concerns or complaints were voiced by the congregation or needs clarified by staff members. We might illustrate some of the group's role functions.

Sounding Board

A pastoral relations committee could provide an informal "sounding board" for the pastor to check concerns with a representative group of his people. Five or six key leaders— elected for three-year terms of service—could convey the wisdom of the church or agency to leaders and, in turn, hear needs expressed and share personal issues with staffers in a private setting. Such consultants could advise the pastor of possible outcomes of proposals, evaluate his concerns, interpret complaints, and offer suggestions for change or improvement. It would act as a buffer, absorbing blows from habitual malcontents.

Viewed as a pastor/staff support group, there would be no formal recommendations, only relational concerns during informal discussions. The group, when motivated, could initiate specific items of business to be brought before the church through appropriate committees. Such a group would work similarly in overseas settings to encourage accountability among missionaries and smooth conflicts if and when they arose.

Conflict Resolution

The church-minister relations committee could serve as a referee in the event of unresolved anger or differences in policy or personal relations. Prevention of crises would be a major responsibility. As a review committee, the suggestions, gripes, complaints, expectations, and compliments of the members could be conveyed to the pastor. Twice-a-year meetings, perhaps in a retreat or informal setting, could provide a relaxed place to discuss such matters in a reasonably defused atmosphere. No one's job would be at stake. His or her work would be reviewed, challenged, and corrected if needed, and warmly encouraged.

The pastor or employee, in turn, is given an opportunity to surface his expectations, frustrations, questions, concerns, hopes, dreams, doubts, and fears with sensitive, knowledgeable, and supportive leaders. Such meetings might provide the pastor a chance to float a few trial balloons to test the reactions to them. From the beginning, the group should be viewed as a support network for both the pastor and his wife. While functional matters could be brought up for review, the committee's particular strength would be relational concerns. Fellowship, not business, would be its chief purpose.

Chaired by a person who is strongly person centered, wise in the history of the church or institution, and optimistic in faith, the committee could effect reconciliation when conflict comes. Two assumptions undergird the previous statement. One, pastors will have problems; the question is not "if" but "when" trouble comes. Two, prayerful, Holy Spirit-guided, wise persons can deal with sticky, even profoundly hurtful, issues when they arise and find solutions together for everyone's best interest. To be effective, however, there must be agreement that the relationship is worth the energy expended and stress experienced in such a resolution process.

A true test of leadership is one's response to and management of conflict. Resolution requires a healthy Christian theology as well as knowledge of conflict management. Much work has been done in conflict resolution to help Christian persons solve their disputes.[11] The Bible itself challenges persons to settle their differences, lay aside angry feelings, and live together in a harmonious fellowship. "Let all bitterness and wrath and anger and clamor and slander be put away from you, along with all malice. And be kind to one another, tender-hearted, forgiving each other, just as God in Christ also has forgiven you" (Eph. 4:31-32, NASB). God's Word does not deny or dodge the reality of conflict, for its roots reside deep within human nature. To live is to have ideas and emotions that, sooner or later, will collide with convictions and feelings of other people.

Lloyd Elder noted that Jesus Christ, who was without sin, experienced differences with His parents, conflict with Satan, and misunderstandings with the religious leaders of His day. It is a "given" of family, organizational, and human existence. "Although conflict has its roots apart from sin," wrote Elder, "there is no question but that sin has added a tragic dimension to conflict."[12] Thus, there is a marked contrast between *destructive* and *productive* conflict. The former is fed by fires of selfishness, ambition, greed, hatred, and desire for revenge. Whereas, productive conflict claims commonality of purpose, mutuality of involvement in events, "weness" of ownership ("We have a problem; let's talk."), prayerful reliance upon God's Spirit, fair consideration of alternatives, and mutually pursued avenues of resolution and future courses of action.

Occasionally, a neutral outside referee must be invited by a church to help negotiate the resolution of conflict. Judicatory officials, associational ombudsmens groups, and impartial denominational consultants can assist with the inventory of concerns held by opponents in a fight. Such third parties have no particular axe to grind with any group, can see larger patterns of ministry rather than single issues, propose alternative solutions, consider possible outcomes of various alternatives, and aid in negotiation of constructive courses of action. A study of biblical patterns, though not fully pursued in this context, suggests the virtue of such consultation (Matt. 18:15-17), wisdom of peacemaking (Matt. 5:9; Rom. 12:18), need for humility (Rom. 12:3; 1 Pet. 5:6-7; Jas. 4:6-7), power of forgiveness (Matt. 6:14-15; 18:21-22), and strength of love—human and divine (John 13:34; Matt. 5:43-44; Gal. 5:14).

Conflict resolution is a faith venture. There are no sure-fire solutions from a human viewpoint to profound problems. Perhaps people who really care will learn to live in peace, despite their differences, and with acceptance, despite their flawedness. Divorce, resignation, termination, character assassination, unforgivenness, animosity, even murder (or murderous desires) are the alternatives. How much better to live on the high ground of forgiveness and trustful acceptance!

Numerous Advantages

The idea of a pastoral relations committee has numerous advantages. People would have a structured, though informal, channel of communication with the pastor and staff. As things stand, many laypersons feel powerless to offer constructive suggestions in churches "run" by the pastor, staff, and committees. Pastors need the wisdom and counsel of trusted, key leaders and the bonding of friendship such a support group might give.

A pastoral or staff relations committee could become a vital link in the supportive network that denominations seek to provide for church employees. Such relational support groups might save many talented, often hurting, ministers and their wives for church-related vocations.

"What if a new minister did not desire such a working arrangement?" someone might ask. The committee could be dissolved whenever there was a pastoral vacancy, if there was no viable reason for its ministry. It could easily be reconstituted after the arrival of a new minister unless the new pastor objected to the existence of such a group.

To summarize, the illustrations I have given include only a partial list of human needs, encouraging signs, and approaches to conflict that may help religious professionals cope with finitude. Considering the price of pastoral/missionary humanity will serve us well as a base from which to offer suggestions about sharing the church's ministry. We turn to them now with the conviction that each member of Christ's body has a ministry. My proposals are offered in the spirit of Christians committed to sharing "all good things" with their teachers sent from God (Gal. 6:6).

Notes

1. James C. Barry, comp., *Preaching in Today's World* (Nashville: Broadman Press, 1984), p. 65.

2. Louis McBurney, *Every Pastor Needs a Pastor* (Waco: Word Books, 1977), p. 57.

3. *Webster's Third New International Dictionary*, 1981.

4. William V. Arnold, *The Power of Your Perceptions* (Philadelphia: Westminster Press, 1984), p. 84.

5. Robert A. Raines, *The Gift of Tomorrow* (Nashville: Abingdon Press, 1984), p. 142.

6. Lyle E. Schaller, *Survival Tactics in the Parish* (Nashville: Abingdon Press, 1977), p. 27. See "Shepherds Who Have Stayed," *Leadership* (Fall 1983), pp. 131-43.

7. *Baptist Standard*, May 30, 1984, p. 5.

8. Ibid., 10 Sept. 1980, p. 2.

9. John Claypool, *Opening Blind Eyes* (Nashville: Abingdon Press, 1983), pp. 55-56.

10. Schaller, pp. 179-92.

11. See, for example, James D. Anderson and Ezra Earl Jones, *The Management of Ministry* (New York: Harper & Row, 1978); Speed Leas and Paul Kittlaus, *Church Fights: Managing Conflict in the Local Church* (Philadelphia: Westminster Press, 1973); Speed B. Leas, *Leadership and Conflict* (Nashville: Abingdon Press, 1982); and Larry L. McSwain and William C. Treadwell, Jr., *Conflict Ministry in the Church* (Nashville: Broadman Press, 1981).

12. Lloyd Elder, *Blueprints* (Nashville: Broadman Press, 1984), p. 175; see pp. 167-88.

7 Community:
Shared Ministry of the Church

Several Christian friends were discussing the leadership and status of a large church that, by theology and tradition, affirms freedom in ecclesiastical matters. Being congregational in polity, it would claim biblical warrant for its very existence and evangelistic ministry.

"When we asked certain members of the congregation about a matter, they said they needed to check with the pastor before replying," noted one discussant. "He speaks for us," was their disclaimer.

"The people are not at liberty to make a move without the church's administrative staff telling them what to do," replied a church watcher who had lived close to the congregation in question. "They claim to be a free church in the congregational tradition, but they function like a hierarchy under a bishop's jurisdiction."

A heavy-handed clergyman had taken control of the church's worship and work more than a decade earlier and had moved it into a split-level polity. A few ordained ministers composing the church's administrative staff were grouped as the "leaders" in charge. The rest of the church was designated as the "people," meaning the unordained people without influence in shaping its ministry. Like many of its counterparts in today's world, the church is divided into two distinct classes of believers. There are the ministers, and there are members to whom the clergymen minister. Such an "upstairs-downstairs" mentality reflects a nonbiblical caste system of superior and inferior Christians.

All that has been affirmed thus far in our discussion runs counter to a ministry based on status rather than service. The New Testament pictures a shared ministry by all believers and those called and commissioned to lead their service. Paul assured the Christian converts of Corinth, for example, that his commission from God was to participate in ministry with them and other "Servants through whom [they] believed" (1 Cor. 3:5-6). Together, they were God's harvest, the gift of His generous grace, and fellow workers for God (see 1 Cor. 3:9). Rather than displaying a party spirit, splitting their fellowship over spiritual gifts and favorite former pastors, the people were expected to serve God in unity.

The Bible does not begin its discussion of ministry with the ordained offices of the church, then descend to the ordinary members. Were that the case, one layman's reputed testimony would appear correct. "My task in the church is to show up, sit up, pay up, and shut up." Many laypersons feel that way, but their impression runs counter to a theology of shared responsibility for total ministry.

To appreciate the New Testament's support of a common ministry, we shall examine first the nature of God's action and the way commissioned ministry fits into His gifts to all believers. Then we shall propose a covenant for shared ministry and list ways laypersons can free their professional helpers to function more effectively.

God's Ministry and Ours

Christian ministry is grounded in the ministry of God who shares it with the whole church for the sake of the entire world. The New Testament affirms that the Holy Spirit empowers all believers from the time of baptism for sharing in his ministry. Paul called this empowerment "the manifestation of the Spirit for the common good" (1 Cor. 12:7). Ministry was defined for the Corinthian Christians in terms of the Spirit's activity in and through the church.

Thomas W. Gillespie, in an inaugural address as president of Princeton Theological Seminary, addressed the subject of God's ministry assigned to all Christian believers. He based his remarks upon Paul's exposition in 1 Corinthians 12, and the commentary of Reformed theologian Jürgen Moltmann, *The Church in the Power of the Spirit.* "Now there are varieties of gifts, but the same Spirit; and there are varieties of service, but the same Lord; and there are varieties of working, but it is the same God who inspires them all in every one," wrote Paul (1 Cor. 12:4-6).

Gillespie elaborated on the trinitarian work of Father, Son, and Spirit in Paul's comments.[1] There are "varieties of working" by God in the world, "varieties of service" by our Lord, through "varieties of gifts" of the Holy Spirit. Three Greek nouns describe God's redemptive work in the world: workings (energies) is from *energemata,* service from *diakonia,* and gifts from *charismata.* The evidence of God's work resides in the activity we see all about us. Diakonic work meets genuine human needs; it is based on lowly servanthood, not status, and involves cost to the giver. *Charisma* implies the grace gift God provides in order that His work shall be accomplished on earth.

Here is Gillespie's point. "If we are to use these three terms as adjectives, then they are properly ascribable to God."[2] Paul holds that God is energetic, diakonic, and charismatic in ministry to and through the church. His ministry continues through the congregation's life and work. Divine enablement is provided to "each one individually as [God] wills" (1 Cor. 12:11).

If it is the church itself that ministers, you may wonder, does the Bible suggest an order of such service? Is there any place for orders and offices of ministry? Paul addressed that question with the metaphor of the church as Christ's body, then noted: "God arranged the organs in the body, each one of them, as he chose" (12:18). In His creative genius, God intended that the body's vital organs and major systems function together with every minute nerve cell and muscle fiber. Each part served every other part to enhance life, health, and usefulness.

Then Paul applied the body metaphor to the reality of congregational ministry. "Now you are the body of Christ and individually members of it. And God has appointed in the church first apostles, second prophets, third teachers, then workers of miracles, then healers, helpers, administrators, speakers in various kinds of tongues" (vv. 27-28). "Appointed" here is the same Greek word (*tithemi*) he used in verse 18, translated "arranged." Just as God arranged the body parts to work effectively, so He appointed apostles, prophets, and teachers to help churches minister well. Orders of ministry developed in the early church—pastors and deacons—in order "to equip the saints for the work of ministry" (Eph. 4:11-12). Leaders, however, were not to usurp the entire church's God-given assignment of mission.

Ideally, the people of God live in a single-level house of shared ministry where family members relate as equals. There is no biblical basis for clergy to live "upstairs" and laity "downstairs" with unequal ranks and privileges. Yes, God provides unique gifts and calls certain persons into ministry vocations, but not into a caste system. A theology of shared ministry views a church family fulfilling its Christian calling, motivated and organized by servant leaders who honor God and respect other Christians.

Formation of Relationships

Having examined a biblical framework for ministry, the issue immediately turns to relational matters between churches and ministers. If believers and their chosen leaders are brothers and sisters in Christ, how are healthy relationships formed? How can ties be strengthened to last and to prevent involuntary terminations like those mentioned in chapter 3? My thesis is that forced terminations are preventable, for the most part, when church-minister matches are prayerfully and carefully formed and patiently and lovingly nurtured.

Durable relationships between pastors and people, missionaries and nationals, are formed in covenants of mutual respect, knownness, fidelity, care, growth through pain, and intention to stay together. Accepting an invitation to become a minister or member of a church staff is similar to a marriage covenant. It is a covenantal agreement to live and work together, under divine assignment, "for the duration." Forced termination is a destructive way to deal with such a sacred relationship under God.

In the United States, church-minister matches are made in what is properly termed the free church tradition. In his book *The Lively Experiment,* church historian Sidney Mead contrasted the free churches of American denominationalism with established churches in Europe. Something happened here in the nation's early life that had not occurred in more than one thousand years of European church history. Free churches emerged in a free state with constitutional guarantees of separation of church and state. Here, no church could be established by the state. Neither state nor church bodies would prevent the establishment or growth of any other churches.

Ideally, Protestant churches function as voluntary associations of individuals, much as the New Testament pictured the body of Christ. "Just as the body is one and has many members," wrote Paul, "so it is with Christ. For by one Spirit we were all baptized into one body. . . . The body does not consist of one member but of many" (1 Cor. 12:12-14). Accordingly, authority and power in the free church tradition rest not with some ruling official as supreme head. Rather, authority rests within a congregation or group of churches which delegate decision making to a representative body. Members can persuade outsiders to join the body. Together, they consent to the constraints of polity and practice upon which they have agreed.

In free churches the local congregation is responsible first to God, then to itself as part of a denominational family. Mead called this principle "voluntaryism," an idea introduced in another connection in the previous chapter.[3] Church-minister relations in a voluntary system rest on the power of persuasion and principle of mutual regard. For example, a congregation must be convinced that a certain individual should be employed as its pastoral leader. When one is invited to candidate ("try out") for the office of pastor, acceptance by that particular congregation must be earned. Such a system subjects placement in many churches to politics, favoritism, and powers of exploitation.

Churches of hierarchical polity, on the other hand, look to a bishop, superintendent, or ruling body of clergy for placement of priests and pastors. Ministers in the Anglican (Episcopal) and Roman Catholic traditions do not candidate for a position to change congregations or advance their careers. Rather, they are sent and serve the church as ministers of Jesus Christ and representatives of a "holy catholic" communion.

Feelings about relationships of churches and their employed ministers range from sentimental to cynical. The appeal here is for empathic understanding of pastoral transitions and the subsequent dislocations experienced by family members. In chapter 4, I implied that pastoral nominating committees do not function alike.[4] Some work in haste, pushing through the search process as quickly as possible. Later, they may live to regret their superficial procedures and clumsily made matches. Other groups spend long hours sorting through résumés, reading letters of recommendation, and rating candidates' sermon tapes. Many committee members seek divine direction. Some treat the process as merely "hiring" a new employee.

However placement of leaders occurs, by assignment or by invitation, the pastoral family must be "adopted" into the local body of Christ. It is the need for the congregation to *be family* to each of its members, including the pastor and his family, that we underscore. As such, church members are more than clientele. The ministry is more than just another job, and divine calling is more than a career. As in a marriage, rather than hiring a new minister, a church promises faithfully to love, live with, and follow God's minister under an assignment from above.

A Covenant to Keep

Conducting a pastoral search is considered by some observers as a congregation's most sensitive activity. While the church proper receives occasional reports of the search procedure, almost no data is provided on persons under consideration. Some feel that "leaking" names might sabotage the search, damage a prospect's ministry if word were to get back to his people, or short-circuit the process if other nominations were received. Others do not wish to disturb the process by divulging secrets "out of school." Neither is competition among candidates desirable.

The evolution of a pastoral call includes assessing numerous factors listed in chapter 4 like: current congregational needs, ministerial "types" in sister churches, constraints in light of past experiences, growth directions, obvious obstacles, and particular qualities desired in a new minister. The search group has a dual role: selecting a nominee *and* telling a prospective pastor about their church. Theirs is a crucial task of detailed talent search, travel, prayer, negotiation, and care for one another as well as God's flock.

Meanwhile, the congregation must prepare itself, like a bride before her wedding, for the coming of God's minister. Together, they will serve the Lord in covenant. One of the wisest ways to get your pastor off to a good start is beginning with a formal service of installation. Viewed as an occasion of vow taking and mutual commitment, the service should be conducted at a stated morning worship hour or a time when maximum attendance might be anticipated. Representatives from the congregation, city government, local ministers' fellowship, denominational office headquarters, and sister denominations should be invited to share the covenant service.

The newly chosen minister will assist in worship planning to help set the tone for this special occasion. Perhaps a veteran staff member, officer of the deacons or elders, or chairperson of the search committee could preside at the ceremonial installation. The pastor-elect may desire to preach, or he may prefer that a respected denominational leader or minister friend speak. Music for such a high hour should be majestic, selected carefully for theological substance, historic meaning, and inspiring quality. Participation by representatives of the congregation and new minister's own family is appropriate.

Here is a suggested order of worship for such a service of installation. It can be modified to meet the requirements of all-sized churches of varied denominational backgrounds.[5] Some groups may have a stated inductional liturgy provided by a regional denominational office. Others may prefer a simplified worship service.

Service of Installation

PRELUDE—Choral Prelude   Selected
Introit—"All Creatures of Our God and King"   *Lasst Uns Erfreuen*
Processional Hymn—"The Church's One Foundation"   Aurelia
Call to Worship and Invocation   The Assistant Pastor
Greeting   Chairman of Deacons
Welcome to the Pastoral Family
   From the Community   Mayor of the City
   From Churches of the Community President, Ministers' Alliance
   From the Denomination   Executive Director
Anthem—"Gloria in Excelsis"   Mozart
THE CHURCH IN COVENANT:
   Epistle—Ephesians 4:1-7,11-13   Officer, Youth Council
   Charge to the Church   Director, Womens' Organization
   *(Please stand and join in the congregational responses)

By our calling of this man of God to be our pastor, we do now enter into a solemn covenant with our Lord and with our pastor that we will faithfully perform the tasks expected of us as members of God's family and of this church. We will remember at all times the things which we have covenanted to perform with our Lord and with our pastor.

With thanksgiving to God for His mercy and goodness, we accept the responsibilities of our covenant.

We promise to be good hearers and to receive the Word of truth which he preaches. We promise to encourage him in his work and to help him in his endeavor to help us, giving the prayerful thought and planning so necessary on our part.

With the love of God in our hearts and a will to worship Him and to learn of Him, we accept the responsibilities of our covenant.

We carry responsibility with him for the spiritual upbuilding of the church. We are his fellow workers. We are laborers together with him. We will pray for him and with him. We promise to make it our particular duty so to provide for him in material things that he may be free to give his time to the church and its wide ministry without distraction or unnecessary anxiety.

With the love of this church and the love of the fellowship of all Christians we accept the responsibilities of our covenant.

We promise, further, to do everything within our power to advance the kingdom of God in the hearts and lives of people in this city and throughout the world. This is a high obligation. It requires that we be good stewards of the time, personality, and material resources which we have received from God and that we exemplify the love of Christ toward all persons whom our influence touches.

With a desire to honor our Lord and to advance the cause of Christ in the world, we accept the responsibilities of our covenant.

Remember always that we are one body in Christ, and every one members of another. There is one body, and one Spirit, one Lord, one faith, one baptism, and God and Father of all who is above all, and through all, and in us all. May the blessing of God be upon us. And now unto Him who is able to do exceeding abundantly above all that we ask or think, according to the power that worketh in us; unto him be glory in the church by Christ Jesus, throughout all ages, world without end. Amen."

*HYMN—"O God, Our Help in Ages Past"   St. Anne

THE PASTOR IN COVENANT:

    Epistle—2 Timothy 2:1-15   Associational Officer

    Charge to the Pastor   (Person Selected by New Pastor)

(Following the charge these questions will be asked by the pulpit guest and answered by the Pastor)

Do you believe that you are truly called by God to this ministry in His church?

    I do so believe.

Are zeal for the glory of God, love for our Lord Jesus Christ, and a desire to share His love and grace with all persons, so far as you know your own heart, your chief motives for entering into this ministry?

    So far as I know my own heart, they are.

Will you be diligent in the reading and study of Holy Scripture and in such other studies as will help you to apply its truth clearly to the lives of those committed to your care?

    I will, the Lord being my helper.

Following the example of that great Shepherd, will you minister to His people in all circumstances, identifying yourself with them in their joys and sorrows, giving special care to those who are ill, bereaved, or otherwise oppressed?

    I will, the Lord being my helper.

Will you help your people to be good stewards of the manifold gifts of God, that every member may be equipped for the work of ministering and that the whole congregation may be built up in love?

    I will, the Lord being my helper.

Will you endeavor to lead a prayerful and disciplined life, remembering your responsibilities as a Christian husband and father as well as the obligations you here assume as pastor to the flock of Christ you have been called to serve?

    I will so endeavor, with God's good help.

"You, then, my son, be strong in the grace that is in Christ Jesus, and what you have heard from me before many witnesses entrust to faithful men [and women] who will be able to teach others also" (2 Tim. 2:1-2).

PRAYER OF DEDICATION   (Person Suggested by New Pastor)
*HYMN—"A Mighty Fortress Is Our God"   *Ein' Feste Burg*
*Benediction   Institutional Representative
POSTLUDE—Fanfare: "All Glory, Laud, and Honor"
                                Based on "St. Theodulph"
    Following this service, you are cordially invited to attend a
    reception in the first floor auditorium honoring the pastor and
    his family.
*Congregation standing

    Given the theological foundation and profound earnestness
of such a service, readers will realize at once that it is more than
a performance. The congregation as covenanter and minister as
covenantee are not merely showcasing "the new boy on the
block." Rather, the service dramatizes formation of a meaningful bond between pastor and people under God. Such a spiritual union is not to be viewed lightly by persons in or outside
the church.

    The appointment service for missionaries who serve in the
United States or in posts around the world cements a similar
covenant. Officals of the appointing agency or mission board
contribute significantly to each candidate's ministry intent
with a convincing challenge. Words of wisdom in the commissioning ceremony provide a postscript to months, even years,
of consideration of missions, formal application, medical examinations, staff interviews, and careful review of board policies and provisions.

    Such a critical transition in the life of a ministry professional
involves leaving and cleaving, much as in marriage. A physician going overseas leaves his or her practice mid well-wishes
and suggestions from colleagues in medicine. Pastors and ministry specialists required to have "hands on" experience prior
to mission appointment experience a "divorce" from cherished
church members. Farewells with family and friends are painful. There is a finality about good-byes where great distances
and cultural transitions are involved. Given resources of inter-

national telecommunications, radio transmission, and jet flight, the relational problems of distance and time have been reduced. Severed ties may grow even stronger through multiple networks of caring companions on the journey of faith.

The promises given to care mutually for one another and to share ministry in the world signal God's workers to move forward. The covenant community bears the mission of the church in its head, the love of God in its heart, and skills of Christian caring in its hands. In mutual respect and support, God's people forge lasting relationships and initiate new beginnings.

A New Beginning

Laypersons must trust the motives of the new minister in their midst *and* the process that brought him and his family to them. Hopefully, the minister's departure from a previous assignment was pleasant. Circumstances in some cases are clouded by questionable behavior in the past or wrong expectations about the new opportunity.

Here, for example, is a clergyman who has mismanaged his personal finances for years. Unknown to the congregation that extended him an invitation to become its pastor was a major debt to a group of men in his former church. He borrowed $5,000 from individuals to clear up small debts as he resigned with a mere promise to pay someday. Having no line of credit, he stipulated in his call to the new community that $5,000 "up front" money be provided in advance, again by a small group of trusting laymen. He intended to retire the earlier obligation, but things did not work out because of added expenses.

The new church fellowship soon realized that it had been victimized by the pastor's gaminess. He and his family were poor stewards of their time, talents, and financial resources. Without being corrupt outright, he became disreputable by withholding his tithe from the church. When confronted by some of the laymen who had advanced him the $5,000 transition loan, the pastor rationalized his unwise behavior by misrepresenting the facts. In order to prevent a major scandal in the church, leaders eventually called for his resignation.

Character disordered persons occupy offices in ministry as in most nonreligious callings. Screening processes by admissions committees to theological schools and ordaining councils detect the more clumsy gamesmen. Clever persons may slip through the net of educational centers and vocational internships. In the case above, the man refused therapy and changed denominations instead. At last reports he had accumulated a new set of financial obligations and was in trouble again.

A new beginning provides an opportunity to acknowledge: "The old has gone; the new has come." A growing minister makes mental notes of mistakes made in prior situations that will not be repeated. He may have lost his temper, for example, with a group of stubborn laymen in a prior church. Now he has learned to practice self-control and devised ways to confront or work around resistance. Previously, he may have committed himself too many ways: church and denominational duties, writing and teaching assignments, conferences and retreats, evangelistic meetings, and overseas tours. Now time is viewed as the coin of the realm. Overcommitting himself may have jeopardized family relations and personal health. He is more prudent and wisely autonomous in meeting approval needs.

Some people get lost between pastors. Their attachment was to the former minister who functioned as a warm friend, counselor in crises, and presider over family festivals (like births and weddings) and tragedies (like illness and death).

You may hear someone ask, for instance, "Where are Van and Marie these days?" Perhaps they have not been regular in church attendance since Rev. Sanchez came as the new senior pastor. Such a question might signal the need to reach out to the Vance Costellos and provide them an opportunity to meet Maurio and Delores Sanchez, a delightful new pastoral family. The temptation of members in such a situation is to overload the new minister with concerns about chronic absentees rather than making calls themselves. As Christ's body, each one has a vital part in the shared ministry of enlisting outsiders, welcoming visitors, and vitalizing dormant members.

Congregations tend to experience "the pendulum effect" during an interval between ministers. If the former pastor or church staffer were too formal and stuffy, for example, congregants will pressure the pastor nominating committee to find a warm, friendly successor who will "make up" for years of cold worship services. Were the previous minister's wife a deeply troubled woman, unable or unwilling to share her spouse's calling, the congregation might expect her counterpart to be vitally involved in various church activities and ministries. Having a passive, laissez-faire-type pastor for years, a search committee might look for a strong leader to guide the church's future direction.

A subtle warning speaks both ways in new beginnings—to pastors and people. Watch the dangers of overreacting responses and exaggerating expectations in light of previous experiences. Without intending to react excessively, one may overstate his or her opinion, become harsh and judmental, or become anxious and insecure with new people. Wrong expectations are often doomed to disappointment. Better to process one's perceptions of past events with a spouse or trusted friend and, if necessary, work through depressed or destructive feelings with a wise therapist. Develop healthful wisdom and avoid isolating new associates by putting them on the defensive. Emotions generated in previous experiences had best be laid to rest, not projected onto new, unsuspecting friends. Avoid belittling prior pastors and fellow parishioners; the truth will come out soon enough.

Fresh beginnings are laced with temptations peculiar to both congregants and staff leaders. Church members are tempted to press new personnel into old molds. One should not expect a young pastor to have his older predecessor's appearance, personality, gifts, outlook, interests, hobbies, mannerisms, strengths, and ministry directions. The incoming staff leader needs freedom to flex spiritual muscles and become all he or she can be under God. Workers change under divine reassignment, retirement, illness, or death, but God's work continues.

A temptation for transferring staff members is to look back to friends and circumstances in some former place of service. Some go back for business needs; others return for professional obligations like weddings and funerals. Nudged by calls from folks who "just want to chat" about things in the former community, a new minister can split his interests looking backward and living forward. As a general guideline, former pastors and staffers should not involve themselves in the work of churches they have left. Missionaries who have resigned must be prudent about returning to the country they love as independents or under sponsorship of a "competing" agency. Ties of friendship may be maintained at the personal level without hazarding havoc in the life and work of a place one has left behind.

Preventive Maintenance

Appointment of a new missionary or minister involves commitment of resources—spiritual and financial. Skimping or unnecessary cutting of expenses in moving and relocating God's servant can be debilitating to the whole family. In the spirit of sharing "all good things" with teachers sent from God, plan with the family about how they prefer support be provided (Gal. 6:6). Mission agencies have established policies and resources to provide adequate, equitable assistance for new appointees.

The thoughtful layperson wishes his minister a smooth beginning and years of trouble-free, effective service. Here are suggestions for church members and mission planners who can help people get off to a good start and stay on course in Christian ministry.

1. Provide adequate salaries, insurance with health care benefits, automobile and housing expenses, and retirement annuities for God's servants. Churches and church-owned agencies and institutions should review salaries of all staff persons each year. A diligent effort should be made to compensate each person justly and fairly. The competence and faithfulness of each employee is thus recognized.

A pastor who had uprooted his family from church, neighborhood, and friends in one state and moved them to a different region of the country expressed gratitude for the new congregation's generosity. "These people have been blessed," he remarked, "and know how to share blessing with their church staff."

The congregation or church entity should provide adequate disability and annuity programs. In the unlikely event some crisis occurs in the health of a minister or spouse, disability insurance might become essential. You may know of some pastor who has developed a debilitating disorder: cancer, Parkinson's disease, heart disease or stroke; or one who has been injured seriously and permanently in an accident. *Finitude* spells human limitations with which all persons must eventually cope.

2. Encourage religious workers to set priorities for work and play, then to establish limits beyond which they will not attempt to go. When "the sky's the limit" and success is the name of the game, life knows no boundaries. One reaches endlessly for the depths without ever touching bottom, for the heights without ever capturing stardust, and for the outer reaches of earth without ever experiencing true community. Isn't that sad? Many religious workers have yielded to God's will and complied with others' expectations for so long they have no idea how to claim territory for themselves.

A cardiologist's assistant once commented upon clergy compulsiveness and lack of assertiveness in claiming time for themselves. "I think ministers experience health problems more as a result of doing what *people* expect than what God expects."

The truth of her observation is born out in testimony by a minister who commented on a lifelong pattern of overextension. His rural family background focused on external job performance rather than internal reflection, self-development, or spiritual transformation. Praise came from doing, not being; thus, he developed a tendency to "do it all" or to "accept it all" in order to keep everybody happy. He did his work and some for other family members as well while at the same time resenting them and his own needs for their approval. Saying no to people became the hardest thing he ever did. But in the nay saying, he made a discovery—he was saying yes to a healthier, more disciplined, and less resentful existence. Getting in touch with the inside through professional help, he claimed the right to rest from labors and work more comfortably in proper rhythm.

3. Point religious professionals to family time with spouse and children. "For this cause shall a man leave father and mother" and, we might add, congregation, children, mission activity, and all work engagements to "cleave to his wife" (Matt. 19:5, KJV). Even one's own children are not to come between himself and his spouse. Home then becomes a place of refuge from the endless demands of work and play, both of which consume energy.

Ideally, one's spouse is one's wellspring—companionate energizer, renewal center, and fountainhead of joy. Pastoral theologian Wayne Oates paid tribute to his wife of forty years in these terms: "Pauline has been to me [a] lifelong haven of rest, blessed interruption of stress, and liberator from my compulsive resistance to rest. . . . She keeps me in touch with God's gift of rest and renewal."[6] With a latter-day openness, Oates has shared his struggle for freedom and wholeness with fellow Christians. Many ministers have yet to learn how to disengage from church activities, feed their own souls, and nurture their companions in faith, hope, and love.

4. Help your minister establish distance between himself and the church or mission setting. Specialists who serve as counselors to ministers and their spouses observe that certain ones frequently stay "in role" even in a therapy group. A man who feels it is expected of him to be a super Christian, perfect father, pious citizen, effective evangelist, and topflight preacher *all the time* stays on edge. Further, if he is a denominational officer or committee member, he may become further alienated from his true self and his family. He may be a part in a drama rather than a person on mission.

A past denominational president was asked to reflect on his life and work at the close of two years in office. The presidency, he observed, had made him a "social schizophrenic." "It is hard to separate when I am president of the convention, when I am pastor of my church, and when I am just myself. Sometimes you feel like your privacy has been stomped on."[7] The man worked wisely to retain normalcy in his life. His intuitive wisdom demonstrated a longing just to be himself rather than a personage, an actor, or resident holder of a prestigious office.

5. Be positive about your church and pray for your minister and his family. When things at church are going smoothly, it is easy to be complimentary and convey regard for the staff team. To dismantle the deacons, committees, elders, or staff, however, when things do not suit you is to build difficulty into life. Fellowship is broken. Your children's teeth are "set on edge" by your own verbal condemnation. Even worse is two-facedness which flatters the staff member publically but shreds him or her privately. In order to sponsor health among pastor and people, it is best to let one's yes be yes and no be no, as Jesus said, than to be a yes-and-no person.

Being upfront with one's emotions fosters a healthy model in one's own family. Then one does not have to "beat around the bush" with a religious worker who is, in fact, an employee of the congregation. One can speak "the truth in love" with the intent of building up both the person and the congregation (Eph. 4:15). Such esteem reaches beyond flattery. It is the positive regard and respectful recognition of pastoral office from one who is a worker together with God (2 Cor. 6:1). Intercession then comes from an honest heart—a friend who seeks to understand and undergird the work of ministry.

There are many benefits to a church or mission family when workers stay and plant their lives in a field of service. In such a bond of fellowship there is greater potential for reaching and ministering to people. There is a sense of continuity in mission and vision rather than a necessity for starting over every few months. In learning to cope with human limitations, ministers and churches can stay together in covenant. Not only is health fostered and fellowship maintained, they can share the rich harvest of ministry together which God provides.

Notes

1. Thomas W. Gillespie, "The Ministry of God," *The Princeton Seminary Bulletin*, 5, No. 1, New Series 1984, pp. 1-8. Jürgen Moltmann, *The Church in the Power of the Spirit* (New York: Harper & Row, 1977), pp. 307-309.

2. Ibid., p. 4.

3. Sidney E. Mead, *The Lively Experiment: The Shaping of Christianity in America* (New York: Harper & Row, 1963), pp. 28-37.

4. See the planning guide suggested by Em Griffin, "Confessions of a Pulpit Committee," *Leadership* (Fall 1983), pp. 106-113.

5. Service of Installation for Dr. Alton H. McEachern as pastor of First Baptist Church, Greensboro, North Carolina, 27 Jan. 1974.

6. Wayne E. Oates, *Your Right to Rest* (Philadelphia: Westminster Press, 1984), p. 93.

7. James T. Draper, Jr., *Baptist Standard*, May 23, 1984, p. 5.

8 Realism:
Seeing Things as They Are

We have examined the ideal of a caring church shared by members and leaders alike. Realism obligates us to speak of life as it occurs in actuality, however, not merely as essential ideal. The contrast between the way Christian life *ought* to work and the way it *is* can be painfully great. Caring for persons whose primary responsibility is delivering care to others requires us to enter their world and experience daily existence alongside them.

Here we shall move beyond superstition, ignorance, or imagination to consider the unfortunate experiences of two ministers whose lives unraveled at the center. Such cases could be multiplied a thousand-fold to document personal needs of professional caregivers. Then we shall face illusions and mirages people have about occupants of church vocations. To complicate matters, these individuals may deny they or their families are having difficulties and refuse help for fear of damaging a reputation or jeopardizing a future job opportunity.

When Life Goes to Pieces

Consider the pain of two ministers who followed each other sequentially in a New England congregation. The first minister moved to this congregation of about one thousand members from a village church. Deprived of parental support in childhood, he evoked an image of intense loneliness in the high pulpit and daily strains of executive decisions and activities.

151

Some people thought the job was beyond his abilities. In order to cope with the impoverishment of what C. S. Lewis called "need love" in his past and to find solace in his single-minded drive for success, he sought friends in a glossolalia group. In time, he encouraged other church members to experience the therapy of emotional release and sense of specialness with God that ecstatic language experiences provided him. "Lines of force" were rearranged, pro and con, among members who supported and opposed such worship practices. Fellowship was broken, and the pastor was confronted with three difficult alternatives: he could quit the ministry, something he was not prepared for; he could stay on and possibly split the church; or he could bid for a new church and take his strong supporters along with him. He chose the last course of action.

Shock waves set in motion by the residual members' accompaning anxiety and negativism at the church engulfed the succeeding minister. Lay leaders had premonitions of doom about *all* ministers because of one man's behavior. Their insatiable desire to remain in control of the church's ministry at all costs bewildered the new pastor. He and the pastor nominating committee had mutually selected each other, expecting the church to move forward. After months of feeling himself trapped in the undertow of the previous minister (who still, incidentally, was in the same city at a new location), he began solitary drinking episodes.

Who was more embarrassed, church leaders or the minister, when he was arrested late one evening for driving while intoxicated? Church members wept as publicity swept the community—unreal—their pastor, a drunk! Alcohol snuffed out the promise of fruitful ministry and left anger and bewilderment in its wake.

Was there any way for congregants to understand the psychic motors driving this pastor's life? The crisis of authority and control, prompted by certain lay leaders' distrust of clergymen and desire that things go well at the church, exacerbated an old enemy. Having fought a lifelong battle with low self-esteem, now in his mid-forties, with one daughter in university and a son in high school, his goal was "making it" professionally. Responsibility for doing ministry at the church was *his*, yet power for decisions and financial support was *theirs*. This reality eroded his sense of worth and enforced feelings of powerlessness. He solaced his loneliness and sense of impotence with a self-administered drug—alcohol.

Naturally ministers do not display such pronounced difficulties at the beginning of their careers, else they would not have been selected for their assignments. What usually happens is that some oppressive stressor (or a series of stresses) or an insoluble crisis crushes a person who already has problems to the point of collapse. How or when the crack-up comes depends on the individual and the circumstances. The symptomatic factors, like tongue speaking in a nonglossolalist church or alcohol abuse, present behaviors unacceptable to church members. Rather than providing pressured leaders therapeutic aid, dismissal becomes an optional "out." The other side of the coin is that some ministers manifest such antagonistic and defeatist attitudes when confronted with their bothersome leadership style or inappropriate behavior that the situation becomes nonnegotiable.

Persons in religious vocations sense early on that the gospel must make its mark in a chaotic world where backup systems on space shuttles sometimes fail, five-year-old children can develop leukemia, 269 lives may be lost in an airline crash (as senseless as the Korean Air Lines incident in which a passenger plane was shot down by Russian fighters in 1983), where patriots still fight religious wars, the year 1997 haunts Hong Kong, young executives die from heart attacks, and innocent bystanders are occasionally shot in convenience store robberies. Missionaries in overseas settings and US ministers understand they were never promised a rose garden. Yet they and the people of God who cherish them as partners in mission face certain illusions.

Illusions and Mirages in Religious Vocations

An *illusion* is a misleading impression of some reality that prompts misinterpretation of its actual nature. One's judgment is based on misapprehension of fact, a mockery of truth. A *mirage*, technically, is an atmospheric phenomenon in which the air appears to move, like water, in ascending waves. The word implies something deceptive and misleading, akin to delusion. The impression of a Maine farmer illustrates humorously the notion of illusions about ministers: "I sure wish I was a preacher. . . . It'd be nice just workin' one day a week!"

Part of making sense of life is exposing illusions and mirages people have about professionals in church vocations. Being honest becomes a helpful act of care in itself. The New Testament speaks of Christians needing to put aside immaturities and games of childhood during which they may have been tossed about "with every wind of doctrine." Rather, Paul encouraged the Ephesian believers, "speaking the truth in love, we are to grow up in every way into him who is the head, into Christ" (Eph. 4:14-15).

An important aspect of disabusing ourselves of illusions is the acknowledgment of their power in our lives. Giving up dated emotions, judgments formed or vows taken in an earlier stage of development, and correcting inaccurate perceptions of reality helps persons rediscover their true stability in God. Checking out impressions and ideas, both of which serve one as facts in decision making, is thus a Christian obligation. What is fact or fiction in the following statements?

Ministers Must Be Strong at All Costs

The denial of one's humanity seems to be an unwritten rule that many ministers of all faith groups live by. One pastor who had experienced a serious health problem, missed four months of preaching and almost died, commented on his plight, "A minister must wrestle problems alone." It was not that he was too good to complain to God or his congregation. The man had been frightened within an inch of his life. But he revealed his culture's role expectations of ministers, priests, and rabbis. When one's faith in God is secure, one is above the need for human care.

Hear the testimony of two minister friends—an older missionary and a veteran pastor—in moments of honest introspection.

Pastor: "How is your work in Indonesia? When will you be heading back?" The missionary explained some of the tensions inside him as he experienced changing roles and strategies on the mission field. He spoke wistfully of developmental changes in his own body and family of three grown children. Nationals, he said, had to be encouraged to transfer their loyalties to new, younger missionary personnel. Part of him was dying, so he grieved with his confidant.

"And what of yourself," he inquired of the pastor, "how are you keeping up-to-date?" The pastor explained that he had considered returning to school for continued education. "But it's pretty hard when you have kids in college and so many expenses." There was a sigh, a shrug, and the explanation that he had decided to go with the flow of church work since he was not too far from retirement. "I know how to preach, how to visit, and how to lead a church even though it wears me out, and I don't have much enthusiasm for it. It's all I know how to do, and it won't be for much longer." Life was not too compelling for either of them.

Two friends had experienced a serendipitous moment of truth at a college alumni reunion by letting their humanness show. Momentarily they would pass, like ships in the night, each entering his world with anxious courage. The missionary knew that he had to appear strong to colleagues in mission meetings during his last terms of service. The pastor changed churches shortly after their encounter and experienced a vitalization of energy and effort for God.

How hard it is for ministers, priests, and rabbis to live on a pedestal of folk imagination like an earthbound god rather than as real persons among other human beings! The pastor who accompanied church youth on a summer mission trip shared driving duties of the van, wore sports clothes as routine attire, and was surprised with the posttrip feedback in families. The common chorus from pleased young people was, "The pastor is just like us! He laughed and joked with us. We sang and prayed together. He even crawled under the van to help fix a flat. Whoever saw a preacher with grease on his jeans!" Rather than being intimidated with reports to their parents, the pastor was pleased to have lived outside a glass box. He felt more human than otherwise.

What if . . . Did you ever play that little game? What if ministers and members of churches could be real with each other, not just once a year on a July 4 picnic but in all seasons? What if a minister who felt suffocated in his church could tell deacons, elders, presbyters, or members of the official board how choked he felt? Perhaps fresh winds of the Spirit could be stirred.

"I feel as if I've been driving with the breaks on for eight years," said an East Texas pastor as he moved to another state. Why must a creative church leader feel his or her gifts would be used with greater effectiveness elsewhere? What if people who expect near perfection in attitude and action from their clergy, who demand winners in financial giving and statistical growth, could say, "For God's sake, your own sake, and ours— be human!" Mattel's toy game *He-Man,* portraying struggles between evil schemer Skeletor and heroic He-Man for control of Eternia, may provide a cultural clue to feelings about our nation's religious leaders.

Ministers Are Above Mistakes

Most persons in religious vocations are thought to have high moral standards and ethical values—above the average Christian. Through the centuries holy men and women have been placed at the beginning of the faith. Laypersons thought their spiritual estate depended upon mysterious powers, charismatic prowess, divinely sanctioned specialness, and self-imposed efforts at deprivation of human needs and discipline of normal drives (like sex). Their mantle has been a heavy one to wear.

The truth of the matter surprises us. Today, for example, the Roman Catholic church in the US is experiencing a dirth of candidates for the priesthood.[1] Many men are no longer willing to accept vows of chastity, enter the extended disciplinary process leading to Holy Orders, and undertake the self-ministry of rigorous spiritual direction. In danger of shortages of qualified priests laypersons are being trained for the diaconate, and priests of Episcopal communions are being courted to consider the Catholic alternative.

Today, we understand that clergy are people, like everybody else, and they will commit sin. The road they travel in professional preparation is arduous and demanding, and their financial remuneration is marginal. According to one report of 432 occupations recognized by the Bureau of Labor Statistics, pastors ranked 325th on the hourly wage list.[2] This places them in the same category as farm workers, cooks, waiters, and waitresses. But on the level of education, pastors rank in the top ten vocations.

With the exception of "Elmer Gantry" types who are unashamed charlatans, most ministers and missionaries live close to God and actively desire his will in their lives. Gantry was the hypocritical preacher in a Sinclair Lewis novel who duped thousands in the name of religion. Do you remember? Gantry had only one sermon with the introduction: "Love is the bright and morning star!" The words about *love* came spouting out, but his life invalidated his pulpiteering. We shrink in horror from such hypocrisy.

Religious guides should be viewed as disciplined thinkers and productive leaders who face temptations, too. "Of course," noted the Episcopal dean of an Atlanta cathedral, "there is a legitimate reason to expect the clergy to be better equipped to handle sin, but there is no reason to expect them to be stainless steel."[3] Here, the Bible comes to our rescue with the reminder that heroes and heroines of the faith were not without character weaknesses and moral failures. The so-called "heroes of the faith" in the great roll call of Hebrews 11 were, actually, persons of "like nature with ourselves" (Jas. 5:17).

The Book of Hebrews names a succession of noble prophets and Old Testament believers noted for their strength of character. But as one has commented, "There is no real pleasure in remembering Moses' fierce anger and his disobedience, or David's infidelity, or Elijah's despair and withdrawal from the struggle, or Jeremiah's resentment of God and his bitterness with his lot, or Mark's cowardice and desertion, or Paul's rejection of him when the next journey was to begin, or Abraham's lie about Sarah, or Jonah's irritation over the sparing of Nineveh, or Peter's denial [of Christ] . . . or the murderous anger of James and John when they are persecuted by the Samaritans."[4] Their stories have been preserved for our edification because they are true, and God has worked His redemptive mission on earth despite their flawedness.

Temptations in the life of today's ministers cannot be glossed over. They are there, not always gross and obvious for savoring by critics, but subtle, gnawing, insistent, powerful. The obvious sins—such as seducing one's secretary or pilfering the poor box—are rare. Rather, ministers may fall prey to power needs, nurse overactive egos, become jealous of successful (often rival) pastors, practice intellectual dishonesty by "borrowing" another person's sermons, and walk the line between ambition, indifference, pride, and self-contempt. Guilt is a constant companion because ethical standards run deep, and ideals are high. No person is loyal to all his or her loyalties all of the time. Thus, the great need to acknowledge oneself as sinner, seek divine pardon, and nourish one's spirit "in season and out of season" (2 Tim. 4:2).

God's Servants Lead Charmed Lives

A mirage closely related to perfectionism is superhumanity in ministry. Some laypersons still assume their minister rides a magic carpet, not a man-made device subject to accidents and mechanical failures, on daily rounds. As one youngster said, looking up at her well-polished preacher behind the pulpit, "He looks so much like Jesus, he gives me the creeps."

Two ministers I know tell of recognizing their flesh-and-blood limits. In Houston, on their way to a baseball game at the Astrodome, Harold and John (we shall call them) stopped at a convenience store to obtain refreshments for enjoyment during the match. Harold remained with the vehicle as John purchased snacks in the store. A thief suddenly accosted the rider, pushed into the car, started it with keys left in the ignition, and kidnapped him. Because his threats promised eventual death, Harold determined to escape from the vehicle as the thug drove him toward the city's outskirts.

"It was jump or be killed," he told friends later. At the risk of injury or, for all he knew, being shot in the back Harold lunged out of the car at a signal light and ran for his life. Viewed later from a safe distance, the entire episode appeared unreal. That his life was spared in that brush with death seemed like a miracle.

Crisis times come in clergy lives when they bounce against the guardrail of some expressway in life, perhaps through no fault of their own, crash at high speed, and burn. Methodist chaplain Carl Nighswonger, of Chicago, died of coronary disease at age thirty-nine. Gifted missionary Roger Thompson, full of promise at thirty-three, was killed when an airliner exploded into the Andes mountains of Ecuador. Theological librarian Charles Johnson, of Fort Worth, died of brain cancer shortly after an aborted consultation with schools in India. He was fifty-five, and the father of two children.

The nine-year-old son of volunteer missionaries living in Harare, Zimbabwe, was killed instantly as he drove his bicycle into the path of a vehicle. He was unaccustomed to the "left side" driving arrangement introduced by British colonialists into old Southern Rhodesia in an earlier era. To the north in Nairobi, Kenya, that same year, missionary parents learned their elementary school-age daughter had been dragged to death in a bus accident. Her clothing had become entangled in the door mechanism as she exited the school bus. Unknowingly, the driver had dragged her along the street and injured her critically. Having visited with her parents later, I sensed they would spend the remainder of their lives in mystery.

Laypersons like to think ministers are spared family problems, like the darkness of a divorce court. It stuns them to hear that bright and delightful people have lost their way, suffered thorny problems, and chosen to end life together. Divorce drains everyone connected with it though there may be an eventual release from suffering. Such failure at the center of life baffles family members and friends. The finality of divorce hangs like an albatross around the troubled couple's necks. Giving up on marriage means acknowledging one's limits. At a deeper level it means risking rejection from a potential support community by exposing one's mortality.

How do laypersons support religious professionals suffering life's traumas? Guidance comes from people in ministry like Dwayne and Bette Martin who shared the story of their son's fatal illness.[5] The Martins' five-year-old son, Jeff, developed leukemia, survived seventeen months through skilled medical care, but died placidly at age seven. The family experienced every emotion—"a continual yo-yo," said Dwayne—crushed by the initial diagnosis; the agony of seeing their son hurting and being hurt (23 injections, finger sticks, etc., in one day) and not being able to ease it; hope that he might be one of the lucky ones that survive; despair over recurrence; the "bittersweetness" of God's presence and answered prayer even when *the* answer that Jeff would be healed failed to come.

And finally, empathy with God, realizing the preciousness of the gift of His Son for humanity's redemption.

God permitted them to feel frustrated and angry, yet not feeling bad about it, reported Martin. One of the things they found hardest to deal with, that provoked inner resentment, was the well-meaning but ill-chosen advice of people who wanted to help.

One person grabbed Dwayne by the shoulders and told him, "Haven't you read in Psalms where it says by His stripes we are healed? You just have to believe Jeff isn't going to die. He isn't going to die!"

"I didn't want them to preach to me," the pastor said. "I didn't need that, especially by somebody who hadn't been through something like this. I resented it."

Their experience suggests approaches to avoid when trying to help. Do not reassure someone prematurely when your assurance is out of harmony with reality. Do not march brazenly into hurting people's lives with insensitive advice. Avoid inappropriate humor. Do not overdo care, overwhelm sufferers with gifts, or create unwarranted dependency on yourself.

"All you need to do is let the person know that you are there, and you love and care for them," the Martins suggested. "One of the best letters we received said simply, 'I care.'"

"Bear one another's burdens, and so fulfil the law of Christ," wrote Paul, to suggest both the spirit and means of caring for persons in the church (Gal. 6:2). The circumstance preceding this principle, which undergirds all acts of care, assumes that Christian individuals can be "overtaken in [some] trespass." The implication is that *any* believer may occasionally experience a crisis, need support during an overwhelming struggle,

and restoration to fellowship by spiritually mature members
(6:1). While sin (trespass) causes suffering, all suffering is not
caused directly by sin. Some crises appear to strike "out of the
blue." Fellow Christians, who themselves have been comforted
by God in their afflictions, are instructed to comfort (strength-
en) others who suffer "any trouble" (2 Cor. 1:4, KJV).

The notion that "God's servants lead charmed lives" makes
it difficult for many pastors to receive care. They have bought
into the illusion of superhumanity. "*Me* need a minister? I *am*
the minister!" they may protest. Still, the congregation reaches
out in acts of prayer, provision of needs, and prevention of
trouble—like financial deprivation—where possible.

Constructive Criticism Never Hurt Anybody

Because the layperson looks upon the church as "his" or
"hers," not the employed staff's, protective feelings prevail
when any threat comes. The threat often appears in the guise
of some proposal to change historic practices of the congregation, remodel a familiar (though worn) education or worship
facility, purchase new equipment, begin a new ministry emphasis, or employ another staff member. Behind the proposal
most often is the pastor. One needing acceptance, support, and
approval finds himself the butt of curious humor, target of
obstructive comments in business meetings, or object of verbal
assaults—frequently from marginal members.

Church members who freely criticize their spiritual guides
think, mistakenly, that "constructive criticism never hurt anybody." Let a seasoned pastor address that illusion on behalf of
his minister colleagues. "When we fear being a failure and our
sense of inadequacy borders on despair, words fitly spoken can
be our salvation [Prov. 25:11]. . . .

The sunshine of kind words calls out all that is best in us,
whereas the darkness of harsh words propels [us] to our worst.
Under the weight of criticism, we often become discouraged,
bitter, resentful and hostile."[6] This pastor, addressing a large

and diverse audience, pled for a spirit of understanding and criticism *with commitment* to ministries of the church. One must consider the source and substance of objections and challenges to his work, he noted, then profit from beneficial suggestions. Above all, one's ministry is offered to God rather than to men (Col. 3:23-24).

Two ministers were expressing concern for a mutual friend who had resigned his church position, then demitted from the ministry. His specialty was music and youth direction.

"Frank's problem was he simply couldn't cope with criticism. He considered every comment as an attack upon him personally. He finally just withdrew into a shell and wouldn't open up to anyone. I think he finally just quit to keep his sanity." Anyone who has served in any capacity of leadership in the church has met with some type of opposition.

We may observe several facts about criticism in the church. One, it is always easier to shoot holes through ministry ideas than to design blueprints for Christian mission. Our Lord Himself stirred controversy by His life-style of compassion for sinners, choice of companions, audacious claims of Messiahship, paradoxical kingdom of God teachings, miracles, and universal evangelical thrust. His severest critics were conservative religious leaders and teachers. Their devout sternness, stubborn resistance to His redemptive dream, and deceptive opposition eventually nailed Jesus Christ to His cross. To repeat, mouthing criticism is easier than proposing constructive alternatives to the status quo.

Two, criticism of persons in any public office is inevitable—politics, education, ministry, the military, or social service. Conflict is an unchanging feature of religious causes. The person being criticized must view his critic's concerns from a positive perspective. "You can't please everybody all the time" is a philosophical way of shrugging off put-downs. To take criticism personally may be to miss the point. One must stay as objective as the situation warrants, dealing with issues and programs, not personalities.

Three, criticism is a sharp instrument. Used as a surgeon's lancet, it might assist in removing troublesome tissue and effecting a cure. Used as a broadax, however, it might bludgeon an object to death. The Bible urges us to guard our lips, as well as our lives, with the reminder of our ultimate accountability to God for "every careless word" (Matt. 12:36).

When criticism comes, four, the religious leader must ask: "Have I proposed some program or committed some offense which justified their criticisms?" If so, one may need to reconsider proposals in conference with lay leaders and make constructive changes where warranted. If, inadvertently, a member has been offended, reconciliation can be negotiated through confession and forgiveness. Does not God's Word help us here? Adversaries are to agree quickly with Christian family members rather than appear in court and become subject to some unfriendly judge (Matt. 5:25). Some criticism, on the other hand, must simply be ignored. Miserable people must not make the minister miserable.

Finally, prayer for one's religious leaders in a spirit of trust, seeking understanding, leads to unity. Harmonious progress in Christian mission is promised to persons who learn to live and work together (2 Cor. 6:16 to 7:4). The terse wisdom of an epigram displayed widely during World War II says it all— "Careless talk costs lives." It did then; it still does today!

Let me list other fantasies about religious work and workers that get in the way of healthy church-minister relations. These mirages of ministry come in many forms and wear curious disguises. To be aware of them may prompt you to investigate their potential impact on the life and work of some pastor or missionary you know. Then we shall conclude our discussion with a major care concern.

Placement Will Take Care of Itself

This myth borders on the magical in religion. It might be viewed as "knight-on-a-white-horse" theology. Ministers are rescued from one place and dropped into another spot. Put simply, it infers that there is a place for every person in religious vocation and a person for every place. Somehow, they get together; everything works and, like fairy tales, have happy endings. In truth, mismatches occur in missions assignments and church vocations as in all other callings.

Terminating Ministers Is a Private Matter

Closely related to opportunity mirages are illusions about pastoral dismissal. Staff tenure differs strikingly from one denomination to another. In denominations like Baptists, Disciples of Christ, and the United Church of Christ, power over the minister is primarily congregation based. When folks become unhappy, they may attempt to freeze out a church staffer by withholding support—emotional or financial—or withdrawing from responsibilities. As a result, a minister may be forced to leave the church.

On the other hand, the Roman Catholic Church and the Methodist Church exemplify hierarchical power over ministers' careers. In these systems power to determine clergy placement, advancement, and tenure lies far more with ecclesiastical officials than with the local church.

Here is the point. A minister's life, family, authority to lead, vocational identity, livelihood, reputation, and future career reside in relationships with laypersons. That structural dependence creates psychic and economic vulnerability for a pastor. His spiritual vision and values do not always click with a congregation's outlook. To terminate such a person, however, is much more a public and profoundly serious matter than many laypersons realize. The kingdom of God in that place is at stake. Issues for time and eternity rest uneasily in human hands. One privately circulating a petition among members or negotiating pastoral dismissal with church officials is answerable, ultimately, to God.

In light of the convenantal nature of church-pastor relations, two cautions are in order. Ministers desiring recognition and advancement from those who have power in the denomination's career system must not jettison their theological moorings. Paul advocates conscientiousness: "From the Lord you will receive the inheritance as your reward; you are serving the Lord Christ" (Col. 3:24). Laypersons, on the other hand, should sense that ministers are under obligation "as serving the Lord and not men" (Col. 3:23). God, ultimately, is the guarantor of one's vocational effectiveness. Thus, one's final faithfulness must be to Him.

Depression Is Punishment for Sin

One sees numerous masks of depression in the ministry and other helping professions: sadness, isolation, anger, alcohol abuse, compulsive work, loss of sexual energy, compulsive overeating, psychosomatic complaints, overuse of prescription drugs, even risky, illicit sexual escapades. We may be more bothered by a person's symptomatic behavior than underlying depression.

A Christian psychotherapist reported his attempt to aid a missionary wife who was having an extramarital affair.[7] Deep down she did not really want to be involved with another man but could not seem to help herself. He recognized in her a deep-seated depression and hypothesized that this was the reason behind the affair. The woman was using a man who found her attractive (and useful for his own purposes) to prop up her sagging ego. As her depression was treated and lifted, her compulsive need for a secret lover's attention dropped away dramatically.

We remember Job and his three comforters in the Scriptures. They sought to link his tribulation with sin. In the woman's case above, depression lead to sin rather than being the punishment for sin. Her need then was for forgiveness: human and divine.

Depressions have numerous causes: some physiological, due to bodily chemical changes (like thyroid imbalance) and disease processes (like brain tumor); some psychological, due to stresses in the life cycle of aging; and some situational, like the loss of one's health, spouse, job, or reputation.[8] Down days, "the blues," and heaviness of spirit, while universal, are special problems for religious persons. We are idealistic, conscientious, even perfectionistic. Guilt feelings consume God's persons when they think they've failed. Depression may *feel* like God's anger for human sin or failure. More likely, it is the mismanagement of one's feeling cut off from God, the loss of approving relationships, that intensifies the pain of depression.

Preachers Should Preach . . .

Most pastors I know would pay dearly for the privilege of limiting their professional functions to preaching the Word and presiding over the ordinances. Daily they are pulled in several directions: homes, hospitals, committees, the church office. Critics who would confine pastors to pulpits usually have a "hidden agenda"; they feel ministers shouldn't meddle in worldly matters. On the other hand, pastors themselves believe in the primacy of pulpit work and scramble for every hour of study time possible. Presbyterian pastor John Killinger expressed such conviction in a book entitled *The Centrality of Preaching in the Total Task of the Ministry.*

Ministers and missionaries are symbolizers of the Christian gospel. Their responsibilities appear global as God's representatives. In establishing priorities, they must learn to delegate certain responsibilities to competent colleagues and say no to some things. Personal and family responsibilities, staff supervision, worship preparation, denominational obligations, building programs, and crises in church families tax their energy and health. Your ministry as a layperson is to share the minister's work load, wherever possible, pray for your pastor, and encourage him to take time for himself and his family.

Ministers Must Leave Monuments
Success Is the Name of the Game

Let me group these two statements together. So often, these "musts"—caught by clergy from Western culture and sought by laypersons with corporate mind-sets—walk hand in hand. Since ministers work with intangibles—conversion of souls and kingdom of God ideals—they cannot easily measure success. One can see, touch, and be impressed with architectural achievements. Buildings change the landscape. They symbolize vitality, financial investment, and concrete effort (as well as indebtedness and interest payments). Billions of dollars are invested globally in temples, cathedrals, social work and retirement centers, hospitals, educational facilities, parish houses, and physical fitness and worship centers. They say to the world, "See! We're here; we care. Come join us."

My concern is not against architecture. Buildings are essential, tangible expressions of a congregation's identity and mission on earth, however plain or fancy they may be. Rather, laypersons must also prize biblical virtues—faith, hope, love— and social values like justice and kindness on earth (1 Cor. 13:13; Mic. 6:8). The Bible's prophetic tradition, including the ministry of Jesus, stands against idolatrous symbols of culture religion. The church's hope, wrote the apostle Peter, is persons whom God chooses as "living stones . . . built into a spiritual house" (1 Pet. 2:4-5). When lay leaders seek first to be "a holy priesthood," offering "spiritual sacrifices acceptable to God through Jesus Christ," their ministers will desire that, too.

Self-Care Is Basically Selfish

Too many ministers and missionaries advocate an inverted theology which puts themselves last on the care list. It runs correctly, "God first;" then erroneously, "others second, and self last." Jesus taught, in keeping with Deuteronomy 6:4, that we are to love God with heart, mind, soul, and strength—our whole selves. Properly, God comes first. Then he added, "You shall love your neighbor as yourself" (Mark 12:31; Luke 10:25-27). His meaning? One must have a gift to give when offering oneself unselfishly to anyone else.

The wisdom of Jesus is born out in modern psychology. A person should accept himself, respect and care for himself, in order to prize and minister to others. The pastor who encounters calls for help and habitually responds, "I just couldn't say no; they needed me" may be victimized by his own need for approval. One who denies himself the care he extends to others is headed for burnout or breakdown of health.

But, someone may protest, are we not to follow the model of Jesus who "emptied himself" and took "the form of a servant"? Paul is further quoted, "Do nothing from selfishness or conceit, but in humility count others better than yourselves" (Phil. 2:3-7). The denial of oneself, setting aside one's interests, and delaying gratification of one's own needs and desires is viewed as the ideal for ministry. Understandably so, since the Christian life itself is a call to take up one's cross and follow Christ. Yet, we need to see the whole picture. Charles Rassieur, who codirects a clergy career development center in Minnesota, reminds us that the resources to accomplish Christian ministry do not come from the servant. Rather, the "power to endure is possible only because Christ himself is the Suffering Servant."[9] He is "the vine"; his servants "the branches. . . . Apart from" Christ we "can do nothing" (John 15:5).

Rather than self-care being selfish it is absolutely essential for effectiveness in missions and ministry. How can laypersons help? Insist that your pastor take his day(s) off weekly, away from the church premises. Encourage him in hobbies that are a clean break from "people problems," things he enjoys where creativity is satisfying. Don't knowingly add to his stress by "talking shop" during a golf game, fishing trip, or dinner engagement. Join him in sports activities—like racquetball or golf, hunting or fishing—he enjoys. Do not insist upon low golf scores or competitive activities which exacerbate compulsivity and extend exhaustion. Encourage family time for the minister's family as well as your own. Honor his need for solitude, request for study time, and polite decline of some social engagements. Call him at the church office rather than at home, except in dire crises. And honor an appointment system in calling if that serves everyone's time needs best.

Providing career assessment, continuing education, personal/professional growth, and therapeutic resources—when such needs are clearly indicated—says "we care." In the event such growth opportunities are needed and agreed upon, financial, as well as spiritual, provision should be assured.

Robert Dale has confessed the destructiveness of stress in his own life. Upon assessment, he composed a list of seventeen needs for his own personal/professional development. Dale called his self-evaluation a "declaration of dependence" and included areas as diverse as spiritual meditation, diet, and weight control in his program. "These renewed priorities," he wrote in *How to Encourage Others*, "helped me feel a greater sense of control over my life."[10] It is precisely such disciplines that aid in recovering one's own self for ministry.

To conclude, gain familiarity with illusions and mirages like those we have considered which distort truth or blind people to reality. Devise your own method for getting to the bottom of some myth which may be damaging a missionary or minister you know. Once you have gone through such a process, the care you offer to your own church staff members will be more fruitful and satisfying. Hopefully, alternate approaches to those suggested here will come to mind.

Notes

1. "What's Behind a Growing Shortage of Priests," *U.S. News and World Report,* June 18, 1984, pp. 43,36.

2. Protestant ministers' pay averaged $20,790 annually in 1984. Ibid., p. 46. See "Many Clergy Couples Threatened by Divorce," *Baptist Standard,* 23 July 1980, p. 16.

3. "No Angels in Pulpit," *The Atlanta Constitution,* Jan. 25, 1976, pp. 1,12.

4. William B. Oglesby, Jr., "Biblical Perspectives on Caring for Carers," *The Journal of Pastoral Care,* June 1984, p. 88.

5. "Trust Is Better than Understanding," *Baptist Standard,* June 1983, pp. 8-10.

6. Bobby Moore, "The World Needs 'Apples of Gold,' " *Baptist Standard,* June 27, 1984, p. 18.

7. Archibald D. Hart, *Coping with Depression in the Ministry and Other Helping Professions* (Waco: Word Books, 1984), p. 50.

8. See my discussion of depression and its resolution in *The Promise of Counseling* (San Francisco: Harper & Row, 1978), pp. 158-173.

9. Charles L. Rassieur, *Stress Management for Ministers* (Philadelphia: Westminster Press, 1982), p. 40.

10. Bill G. Bruster and Robert D. Dale, *How to Encourage Others* (Nashville: Broadman Press, 1983), pp. 20-21.

9 Commitment:
The Power of Family Life

Starting out in Christian vocation, young ministers anticipate that time is on their side, that success in work and family living will reward true effort, and that, with God's help, any crisis can be mastered. In young adulthood, the future stretches before individuals endlessly. They imagine they can compensate eventually for anything they missed earlier. While such optimism is commendable, it may blind immature professionals to a fundamental reality. Some family experiences cannot be neglected, delayed, or bypassed repeatedly without irreparable damage to relationships. Successful families, like successful individuals and organizations, require careful planning, profound trust, clear communication, mutual effort, and forgiveness of mistakes. Such commitment undergirds effective family life.

Incidents of ministry marriages that failed bear witness to family values and needs for which there are no substitutes. The aspiring theological teacher, so married to his lectures and scholarly activities that his wife endured living with him *in absentia,* discovered regrettably he had pushed her beyond the point of no return. His sponsoring missionary organization called for his resignation when news of their divorce reached the home office. An investment in theological education and preparation of almost half a lifetime ended on the ash heap of failure and regret.

Many ministry marriages reflect the traditional hunter-and-gatherer imagery, with husbands providing the primary source of income and spouses managing the home front. Wives who outgrow or become dissatisfied with such an arrangement have few options: adapt and continue to submit, develop a separate career, or terminate the marriage. Complementary partnership is a viable biblical alternative.

A minister whose wife was expecting their second child was shattered by her premature death. She became critically ill while he was out of town for an evangelistic meeting and suddenly died. Later, he married a woman with children and thought he was a responsible partner in the new, blended family. But the second marriage withered under continual pressures of his achievement-oriented life-style. Because his spouse sensed after years of effort that his career meant more than his family, she moved out. His divorce led eventually to loss of effectiveness in a major church organization.

Another minister discovered there was no way of double-talking his way out of missing the birth of his third child. His wife gave birth to a son while he was out of the state on a hunting trip with friends. His spouse felt there were some family events requiring priority, and childbirth was one of them. The grudge she held against her successful pastor husband hardened into resentment, then hatred, and finally divorce. He had been missing in action too many times previously including absence during an earlier child's first birthday. His neglected spouse felt that other persons and events were number one in his life, thus she divorced him. With home and career in shambles, the minister left his congregation and started over in another part of the country.

Laypersons collaborating in family and church life with their religious leaders will keep in mind the close relationships between a minister, his family, and church organization. Life functions dynamically like interlocking circles. What happens in one area affects relations in other areas, so they are never in static balance but always in dynamic tension. In each situation

Dynamic Relationships

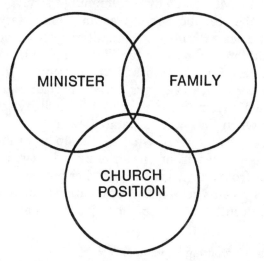

a minister/missionary needs the guidance of priorities in order to determine his investment of time and energy.

Strengthening family living for church and mission professionals involves the perspective of a wider vision. Imagine yourself for a moment trading places with some mission family member. Try to "feel" your way into his or her shoes.

Mission Families: Trading Places

Sometime ago my wife and I were involved in teaching East African national theological students courses in the area of marriage and family relations. During the year we were invited to share special occasions that had a uniquely American flavor with fellow missionaries. En route to Africa we shared a July 4, Independence Day, picnic with mission friends in Israel at a spa reportedly developed by Romans during the era of Herod the Great. In November, for example, we enjoyed a Thanksgiving Day covered-dish dinner with missionary "family" members. The weather was warm enough in the Southern hemisphere for the MKs to enjoy a swimming party.

Through the year there were wedding anniversary celebrations for couples with lifelong commitments, birthday parties for children, farewell teas for families going on furlough, and welcoming teas for distinguished visitors and newly arrived missionary personnel. We experienced the gladness of parents collecting MKs from boarding school for holidays and pangs of sadness when they were separated again.

You can discover a bit of what it's like to be a third-culture kid, living separated from one's family overseas, by reading this excerpt from a teenager's note to her parents. Kay Sperry wrote to her parents in a Third World nation upon the occasion of her seventeenth birthday. She had just returned to boarding school.

> Thanks for wanting September 3 to be *special* for me. It was! There were no festive balloons or colorful nosegays of flowers, no music records given by friends. Just being together is what mattered. I enjoyed having Jeanie and Bev over for the night. And the jeans dad brought me from the States were on my "most wanted" list. I'm wearing them today!
>
> That you are making it possible for me to visit prospective college campuses in Virginia, at Christmas, is too good to be true. It'll give me a chance to talk with Rennie [her sister] and Sam. And you know I want to be with Ray [a fellow MK friend, already in university]. Who knows?! . . .
>
> Most, I want to thank you and dad for being you. . . .

What was the difference in Kay Sperry's birthday and teenage celebrations in Des Moines, Atlanta, Rockville, or Buckeye, USA? It was not a difference in the honoree's intelligence, basic good looks, health, or economic status and that of average American kids. Her parents viewed themselves as ordinary people. Dan and Liz Sperry had weathered some storms in their twenty-seven years of marriage, including the deaths of two children and close family members. Rather, Kay had been ushered into internationalism as a child. She belonged neither to her home state of Virginia nor to the primitive culture of her parents' adopted country. Kay was marked by her third-culture perspective.

The passing of time would hasten her eighteenth birthday and severing of strong parental ties. Then Kay would be catapulted halfway around the world to an American university. Already she was experiencing the separation anxiety of being launched into life—ready or not—ten thousand miles from her parents' missionary residence. Legally an American citizen, Kay was African in her heart. Her feelings about the future were mixed-up and confused. She faced the future with genuine trust in God and profound reliance upon her parents. Their commitment to each other and to God furnished the glue that held her emotional world together.

Missionary families, like all families, change all the time. While mission life is not constantly beset by crises, and the joys of overseas ministry are real, hazards and heartaches cannot be avoided. Laypersons who tune in to mission family needs will:

• Recognize missionaries work in changing, often risky, historical and cultural environments. Many so-called nonaligned nations where they live and serve endure endless guerrilla warfare, face strong-arm tactics by militant government leaders, and experience a pro-Marxist mentality in one-party socialist states.

• Sense that Christian missionaries work as a radical minority in non-Christian and non-Western lands where white supremacy is dying or already dead. They live against the tide, as outsiders, in order to offer the gospel to people who live in darkness.

• Know missionaries are uprooted from their historical foundations. They are faced with almost insurmountable needs—

like crime, hunger, and suffering—and are confronted by tribal or cultic patterns of family life.

• Support members of mission families, like Kay Sperry, when they return to the United States for education, emergency medical treatment, or furlough experience. Such support must move beyond cosmetic care. It should take tangible form of housing, automobile provision, and meaningful acts of friendship like hospitality during holidays. Reentry can throw mission families off balance.

• Help missionaries overcome the temptation to act like unnormal, all-holy, fully wise, supersaints. Such inhuman qualities are part of the fantasy world some laypersons place upon them. They are often forced into isolation, withdrawal, or lonely hypocrisy rather than being permitted a fully human existence.

• Befriend their aging parents in America, as well as their college-age children. Do not withhold care just because an MK may resort to drugs or alcohol or get into relational difficulties. They may deny care needs, yet long desperately for help from trustworthy Christian persons.

The capacity of friends to experience marker events in other people's lives differs in matters of degree. Some individuals are more perceptive than others. Some have heightened sensitivity to suffering because they are what Henri Nouwen described as "wounded healers" themselves. Psychiatrist Gerald May reminds us, "God calls people of varying degrees of capacity to be spiritual helpers for others."[1] Spiritual ministry calls for an enlargement of such capacities with the help of God's Spirit, prayerful reflection, and wise consultation during one's work. One such marker event is moving to a new workplace. Consider the impact of relocation on ministers, their spouses, and children.

Dislocation and Relocation

"We're going to Kansas City!" There was excitement in the young pastor's voice as he called to thank me for writing several letters of recommendation in his behalf. "Dorothy has already discovered some women in the church who will become her friends. . . . They have a housing allowance, so we'll be able to own our own home again." He was moving from a semirural to an urban setting.

A constant concern of ministry families is dislocation and the insecurity of relocation. Statisticians indicate that Southern Baptist pastors move, on the average, every twenty-eight to thirty months. Some church staff members move more frequently than that. With over 61,600 ordained ministers, plus 12,340 prospective candidates currently enrolled in SBC theological schools, the economic and emotional price tags of minister dislocation in that one denomination almost defy description.[2] And that's only one of more than 250 Protestant, Jewish, and Catholic bodies in the United States.

Think about this for a moment. Imagine you are going to move sometime during the next year, take a different job, pull up stakes, sell your house, pack your belongings, and head for a new setting. Your work world will be new with different associates and assignments. You will live in a different house with strangers as neighbors, and your children will enroll in new schools. In one recent year, 1.2 million American heads of households moved their families from one job market to another. Demographers note the odds are one in five that you yourself may move sometime over the period of the next year.

What do you see with so many moving vans and truck rental vehicles in front of ministers' houses? Broken attachments at work, school, and church? Out-of-pocket costs to the moving companies? What about possible loss in equity values of homes in certain areas of the country? Forced moves, because of involuntary terminations, are usually temporary and must be repeated again soon.³ When that happens, spirits are bruised—some permanently. Some ministers face financial disaster by having to make two house payments if previously owned property does not sell for six months to a year.

People you know have likely lived in a few congenial places close to their geographic and cultural homes. Snapshots of most ministers and missionaries, on the other hand, would picture people in transition, possessions in cars, trucks, and shipping crates.⁴ Rootlessness, in turn, erodes relationships, causes grief, and turns persons inward for self-discovery and support. God's call and a shrinking globe have played havoc with the religious worker's sense of place. *Family* for most of them goes beyond blood relatives to spiritual kinsmen; it also crosses racial and ethnic boundaries.

Consider the experience of Rebekah Naylor, a single missionary surgeon in Bangalore, India. Impressed years ago to leave her family in America, Dr. Naylor's commitments are to God, her patients, and to her hospital/church associates in a land of over seven hundred million people. The mission *family* in India is quite small—a band of scientists and medical specialists. Furloughs take about one third of the staff back "home" to America during any given year. Those left on the field must pick up the extra load from those leaving. Work in the churches—including literacy programs, evangelism, discipleship, and preventive health care—is expanding rapidly. Visiting evangelists from the United States have helped to reach many persons for Christ, but they are not permitted to reside permanently in India and disciple converts. Congregationalizing tasks become missionaries and nationals' challenging responsibilities.

As we consider the almost overwhelming tasks such scientists and medical specialists have taken into their hands, we discover disturbing things about ourselves. Middle-class Americans find it painful to reexamine their past assumptions. To do so is agonizing and threatening. Thus, many Christians remain locked in to their prejudices and provincialism. Theologian Robert McAfee Brown challenges our restricted vision: "Middle-class assumptions we have inherited are not open to reexamination, masculine prejudices must be retained unexamined, white perspectives dare not be compared with nonwhite perspectives."[5] In the churches, are we *for* whoever preserves things unchanged and *against* whatever or whoever suggests change? Can our ears hear cries for medical aid, food to go around, or freedom from tyranny and injustice from oppressed peoples?

To become aware of such restricted vision provides a way to gain freedom from it. But not the full way—the recognition may lead us to dig in our heels and hold on to our resources. Gaining a wider vision comes not by human effort alone but also by the grace of God. If laypersons are to support their own helpers, a good place to begin is with pressures minister families face.

Pressures on the Minister's Family

We have been urging that thinking about care starts with and from within the Christian *koinonia.* In the fellowship of believers, it makes sense to talk about families and what it takes to keep human life human. However, the relationship between professional helpers and those who seek their help is an ambiguous one. Many laypersons are more impressed with ministry greed than need. They relate ambivalently to professionals who appear ready to save others but are unable to save their own family members' integrity.

Religious leaders generally enjoy their family relationships and find rich satisfaction in parenting tasks. This despite the fact the church often becomes the "other woman" in husband/ wife relationships, and that breeds spousal resentment. Balancing career and family can be a tricky business, especially for the new breed of minister fathers who take both roles seriously. Ministry children, in turn, relate to Christian vocation according to their own individual sense of identity and commitment to God. Regrettably, some sons and daughters have been destroyed through their father's ambition. We are encouraged, on the other hand, with reports of high achievements by ministers' children, more of whom are listed in *Who's Who* than offspring from any other vocational group in America.

Some pastors want out of bad situations and see divorce as their final step to freedom. According to the US Census Bureau, there are over 1.2 million divorces each year in this country. The minister's and missionary's marriage has not escaped this undertow.[6] When clergy couples divorce, their actions confront churches and denominational employers with difficult and significant policy decisions. Attitudes toward divorced ministers are changing, perhaps softening in some quarters. The adversity of a broken home, however, afflicts not only the immediate family members. It infects the church organization and prompts loss of public confidence in one's ability to lead other families.

Hidden Pressures

One pastor said, "Our family faces the same pressures, stresses, and strains other families face, only more so." He was partly correct as he thought of economic stresses, working wives and the pressures of dual-career marriages, aging parents' needs for care by middle-aged sons and daughters, and the challenges of launching children into their own careers.

The new feminism and changed sex roles concerning leadership and power in the home cause conflict for some ministry couples. Attitudes regarding husband/wife roles exist along and at both ends of a continuum, according to cultural conditioning, personal preferences, and theological convictions. Concepts about the hierarchical (traditional male dominance) and companionship styles of Christian marriage vary. Partnership is preferred over patriarchy by many spouses.

Psychiatrist Barrie Greiff, of the Harvard Business School,

and his colleague Preston Munter, of the Harvard Law School health service, have identified some executive marriage patterns applicable to ministers. While less obvious to outsiders than the above stressors, their effects may be more insidious.[7] One such hidden pressure is the husband's unrealistic expectations of his wife to aid his rise to the top. To paraphrase Greiff, some young ministers "select a mate" instead of marrying a person, then seek to use their partners as vehicles to serve their own career needs. Such *use* may be of her family status, beauty, capacity as a hostess, intuitive wisdom, professional education, ability to support his unconscious dependency needs, vocational skills, or her ability to "meet the needs of the church." The basis of the husband's choice is his wife's ability to escalate his career objectives. Such a strategy frequently fails for obvious reasons: It prescribes the wife's total functions and future, leaves her no bargaining room for negotiation or trade-offs, and depreciates her self-esteem.

The woman who discovers herself in such a marital trap feels unchristian because of her anger and outrage, unappreciated for her true worth, and unable to mature toward the goal of womanhood she prizes. Divorce is often inevitable. The alternative is a stalemate in a stifled family relationship where one spouse thrives, and the other dies inside. A spouse who discovers that she is always having to go along with everything her husband expects needs power to ask for understanding for herself. Such power can come from God, yet may be actualized through professional counsel and guidance.

Another difficult ministry marriage emerges when one partner outgrows the other. Typically, we hear of the professionally educated husband who has outgrown his wife. She may have worked in order to send him through school and delayed parenting tasks. Now, at home full-time with the kids, she does not have the challenge of keeping up in her field or his. On the other hand, some clergy wives may feel they have outgrown their husbands. Their interests range wide, beyond the home, to social and cultural events, recent books, music, art, and the theater. Some wives are avid sports fans. They take advantage of opportunities to develop themselves personally, often in ways and areas their minister husbands don't pursue. At social gatherings, some wives are embarrassed by their husbands' ignorance of current events and lack of genuine sophistication.

A third hidden pressure on ministry couples is the feeling their marriages must model a perfect ideal. They mistakenly sense they must "keep the lid on" when differences arise. Any slip up in their "piranha bowl" existence embarrasses them. A small faux pas feels like an unpardonable blunder. When strong wills clash and hurts arise, wives particularly feel cut off from sharing with other church couples. The husband may turn to a supportive staff member for emotional release and fresh insight. The wife may feel angry, misunderstood, used, yet cut off from understanding friends. Such private pain, unrelieved, produces physical symptoms, depression, and other emotional disorders.

Medical consultants Greiff and Munter suggest trade-offs as a helpful method of negotiating differences and resolving conflicts in complicated work-family dilemmas. In our case, ministry family members can learn to give up something desirable for another benefit or advantage regarded as more desirable. Rather than resenting having to break in to a vacation for a funeral, for example, a clergy couple should trade up in advance for a staff member to cover such crises. If required to return early, a pastor might request a second vacation later that same year. Another trade-off might be a study leave, with longer vacation period, the following year. Such actions are motivated by integrity not selfishness.

Trade-offs are guided by the values and priorities of pastors, family members, and church organizations. Some personal needs are not negotiable for ministry couples—like an anniversary celebration or requirement of health care benefits. Trade-off situations inevitably involve dilemmas in decision making. Some matters lie outside the minister's control. The goal is to achieve fairness for all three parties—minister, family, and church organization. Laypersons guided by their religious leaders' spirit of servant-leadership can help them resolve dilemmas and achieve satisfaction in complex work-family matters.

Unique Stressors

In the past decade numerous researchers have delved into problems uniquely related to ministry marriages.[8] My own investigation, conducted by questionnaires to several hundred ministers, netted twenty areas of major concerns. Responses came from 206 ministers in three age/experience groups: one to five years in the ministry, five to fifteen years, and over fifteen years of ministry experience. A composite summary of their responses appears in the accompanying table (see Table 1).

The top twenty areas of stress included personal, career, and family concerns. The linkage of personal/professional issues in ministry is intensified since one's faith is also one's work. The percentages reflect composite patterns of stress in religious vocations from three age/experience minister groups. We can highlight certain concerns which make it particularly difficult for ministers to fulfill their obligations, under God, to their churches, families, and themselves.

One, the work of ministry is a gloriously impossible task which must be performed within the rigorous, often merciless, constraints of time. Time is the coin of the realm. As the leader and caregiver for an entire congregation, the pastor feels pulled in many directions. Add to leadership tasks the responsibility for hospital and convalescent center visits, weddings, funerals, crisis counseling calls, denominational meetings, and social events and one can understand the difficulty of finding time for work, play, and family (items 1, 2, 3 of the survey). The effec-

Table 1
Problem Areas in Ministry and Marriage
Items Checked by Three Groups of Ministers. Overall Percentages Reflect Problems in Life and Work.

Item	Percentage
1. Finding time for pastoral duties	76%
2. Creating time for personal recreation	72%
3. Finding time for my family	69%
4. Dealing with criticism from church members	68%
5. Continuing professional education	63%
6. Handling lack of congregational loyalty	50%
7. Responding to unrealistic expectations	58%
8. Facing feelings of professional inadequacy	47%
9. Exercising pastoral authority	47%
10. Handling job dissatisfaction	44%
11. Dealing with finances	43%
12. Facing difficulties with staff members	37%
13. Facing the need for perfection	37%
14. Experiencing clear family communication	37%
15. Experiencing and expressing emotions	36%
16. Conquering sexual temptations	33%
17. Clarifying my pastoral identity	32%
18. Dealing with low self-image	31%
19. Coping with loneliness	30%
20. Developing meaningful personal friendships	27%

tive minister must be guided by definite purposes and priorities in order to move beyond a desperate juggling act toward a harmonic whole career.

Exasperation is the local pastor's daily bread. "Look at this stack of phone messages," a pastor held a fistful of paper slips in view. "I was out of the office a few days last week. Now, I have fifty-two 'call back' messages requiring attention this [Monday] morning!" The mid-fifties minister of a 2,500 member congregation appeared ready to throw up his hands and quit. He had already shared frustrations about two recent staff resignations and the trouble and time replacements would involve.

"A touch-tone phone can save me hours of time in the run of a week," he added. "It's so much faster than dialing." The man was an orthopedic patient who had recently experienced a coronary bypass procedure. I sensed he was mismanaging pressure by failing to make use of an administrative secretarial assistant. Some staff aides pass on all requests, inquiries, and calls for help to the pastor. His desk is the central communications center for the entire congregation. Wiser pastors organize and educate assistants to channel calls to competent colleagues, so they receive basically executive level messages.

How can laypersons help? you wonder. You can aid your pastor by encouraging intentional acts of ministry. Suggest he take time in the early months of a new pastorate to study the church's history, cultural setting, and ministry styles of predecessors. Encourage him to envision with lay leaders the dream God has in store for your renewed ministry together. In the past, he may have developed coping styles aimed primarily at using the rapid relocation system in denominational life. A forty year career, viewed in retrospect, may look like a disconnected series of places of service, glued together by a denominational retirement plan. Surely the ministry is more than *that!*

Redreaming the dream of God's plan for your church requires openness to the process of change, vulnerability to input

from numerous sources, and willingness to face conflict and
negotiate differences as they arise.[9] In moving to a new church
setting, the pastoral family has likely determined whether or
not change is possible with the search committee. The approach suggested here is to place day-to-day acts of ministry
within the framework of long-range vocational and congregational goals. In this way, the minister is able to say no to some
demands and yes to others that flow out of agreed-upon purposes. A supportive constituency, in turn, gathers around the
leader who clarifies his or her views of the purposes of the
Christian faith.

Given priorities and action plans to achieve objectives, a
minister is freed to pursue duties in a deliberate manner. He
approaches life more as a ship's captain, steering by the stars,
than as a resident fireman rushing to fight fires. Lay ministry
team members can share pastoral care opportunities of house
calls and nursing home and hospital visits. Wisdom will dis-
courage his taking an excessive number of extra, out-of-town
engagements. With the family included in preparation for
separation, extended trips need not jeopardize their bonds of
commitment. Rapid means of transportation and communication can keep them in close spiritual and emotional touch.
Sometimes, vacations and engagements go together.

Two, critics also live in the household of faith. You will
recall our discussion about censure and judgment of ministers
and missionaries in chapter 8: "Constructive criticism never
hurt anybody." There's just one thing wrong with that logic.
It isn't true! Items 4, 6, 7, and 8 of my survey deal with issues
of congregational integrity, expectations, fairness, and loyalty.
When expectations are unrealistic or criticisms seem uncalled
for, the grass begins to look greener in other fields. How can
you help?

Cradle your pastoral family members in supportive, patient,
and affirming care so that they, in turn, may be secure and
supportive with one another. When differences arise (as surely

they will in voluntary organizations), confront the clergy's myopic vision or mistaken wisdom. There is no need to push him or her into a guilt trip for being human. The New Testament calls this way of confrontation "speaking the truth in a spirit of love" and suggests that conflict, handled thus, permits us to "grow up in every way into him who is the head, into Christ" (Eph. 4:14), who is the head of the church. Who knows? Your ideas may be more alike than unalike when you process them prayerfully together.

Help to spare church staffers and religious leaders in non-parish assignments from unkind or unjustified criticism. Most ministers can deal with differences or disappointments when we are up front with them about any concern. Before repeating information, check out the source; get the facts straight. They may be rumors which die hard. Having one's motives analyzed, dissected, and reproved, especially behind one's back, is counterproductive. Rather than changing a minister's behavior or achieving a critic's goal, criticism sets both parties up for another round of rejection.

A minister who is exposed chronically to the physical, spiritual, and emotional suffering of his constituents does not need to bear the added grief of criticism. It's cruel to assassinate the character of a meritorious minister or member of his or her family. The Bible calls such judgment sin (Matt. 7:1-6). Furthermore, it's risky for the critic, not merely the one being judged. Should you overhear distorted facts or peevish gripes from grouchy or frustrated laypersons, try to get to the bottom of the issue(s). Encourage them to speak directly with the staff member involved and negotiate their differences in Christian love.

Three, another concern impinging on the minister's family health is his unclear sense of identity and authority. Item 9, the proper exercise of pastoral authority, was checked by 47 percent of all respondents. Item 17, clarifying one's personal identity, was checked by almost one third of 206 respondents.

Several problems in areas of interpersonal relations and job satisfaction reside on the scale between those two items. Note that the focus reported is *frustration* with concerns like: one's job, money, staff differences, and perfectionistic expectations by one's congregants. Conflicts in ministry inevitably become problem areas in one's marriage and other relationships (see items 14-20, Table 1).

Managing one's health is problematic because there appear to be few outlets when things anger the religious worker, when people or events seem unpredictable, or when associates expect him to produce positive statistical results.[10] Every activity is measured against time and the bottom line of success. Trying to fill the role one is expected to "play"—pulpiteer, evangelist, promoter, perfect partner and parent, sensitive counselor, and knowledgable citizen of the world—can be destructive. Better to *take* a role intentionally—particularly the biblical one of servant-leader—than to play one in inauthentic fashion. Hypocrisy is a heavy mantle to wear. Continuing lack of exercise, rest, and quietness may lead to exhaustion, impatience, collapsed idealism, and depression.

Ministers seek relief from such stressors in weird ways. They learn to hide or avoid parishioners by getting on denominational committees, studying harder, running faster, leaving town, or by trading off one task against another. No one suggests an annual psychological checkup, simply a physical examination. Pastors know about pressure. They are concerned about the quality of their lives, but they are also determined to squeeze everything in. As ministers try to thrive in high-pressure, fast-paced jobs that often demand more time and energy than they can muster, they also try to be successful fathers. And it isn't easy—especially since most men are learners when it comes to parenting. So, you wonder, what alternatives are possible?

Possibility Thinking

"If I stop and think too long about all of these pressures and grim problems," said one minister's wife, "I get depressed. Is there any way for me to gain a sense of fulfillment as a person while helping my mate survive and grow in his calling?"

The answer is a qualified yes. At the outset of this discussion, we noted certain qualities of a successful marriage, like shared planning, basic trust, honest communication, hard work, and true forgiveness of mistakes. Guilt is unavoidable when one's marriage fails to measure up to such ideals. It's best to acknowledge it and talk things out together.

The rock-bottom foundation upon which a durable home may be built is commitment—to God and to each other. Two persons, with conflicting or complementary characteristics, can build a life together with raw materials of mutual respect, fidelity, care, fairness, and dependability. Self-fulfillment is a dominant goal of Christian marriage—being all one is meant to be as a person in Christ. Thus, meaningful existence is just as important as financial security for Christian couples. Both spouses must be sensitive to such concerns.

Laypersons who share ministry with their religious leaders desire successful families themselves. Let's think of possibilities for strengthening family life in church and missionary settings.[11] Being a Christian family means:

• Placing one's life, marriage, and family in God's hands day after day after day, trusting His care in all events and circumstances, and sharing His blessings with each family member.

• Building relationships on a foundation of honesty, care, time together, shared activities, open discussion, and mutual forgiveness.

• Enjoying each other's successes and being supportive when one or the other partner fails.

• Hearing one's spouse when he or she is hurting and making

essential changes in life-styles to help the partner cope effectively.

• Sharing each other's private life, yet recognizing that some aspects of personality may remain forever private.

• Permiting unique interests and activities to emerge and thrive as spouses age, change, and grow. Multiple centers of interest, including different career tracks, may enhance growth and enrich marital relationships.

• Coming to terms with one's spouse as a real person rather than living with a fantasy or forcing someone into false roles.

• Establishing a sense of interdependence and at the same time allowing each other the freedom to grow.

• Protecting the family as a unit against the disruptive forces sometimes imposed by community or church or mission assignment.

• Sharing parenting tasks in light of one's preparation, gifts, sex role expectations, interests, and agreed-upon responsibilities within the family system. Also, being consistent as parents.

• Keeping fit in all respects so that one possesses reserves of energy to handle schedules that are frequently overloaded and face crises when they arise.

• Relating life to God for nurture, strength, and forgiveness.

• Scheduling some time for themselves as a couple that remains inviolate and permits them to catch up with themselves.

In ways such as these, Christian persons adapt to life's pressures and grow from "grace to grace" together under God. They look to Him meanwhile for peace and gladness in the pursuit of His will as "heirs together of the grace of life" (1 Peter 3:7, KJV). This leads us to consider how caregivers trust God in the seasons of life.

Notes

1. Gerald G. May, *Care of Mind, Care of Spirit* (San Francisco: Harper & Row, 1982), p. 102.

2. According to the 1984 *Yearbook of American and Canadian Churches* (Nashville: Abingdon Press, 1984); and *Quarterly Review,* July 1984.

3. From chapter 3 you recall estimates of 2,500 SBC church staff ministers being dismissed annually.

4. According to *Quarterly Review,* July 1984, Southern Baptists employ 3,792 missionaries in the United States, and 3,332 career and special-term missionaries overseas.

5. Robert McAfee Brown, *Creative Dislocation—The Movement of Grace* (Nashville: Abingdon Press, 1980), p. 113.

6. While a study by David and Vera Mace, *What's Happening to Clergy Marriages?* (Nashville: Abingdon Press, 1980) was devoted to strengthening clergy couples' relationships, their research turned up many couples in conflict and crisis.

7. Barrie S. Greiff and Preston K. Munter, *Tradeoffs: Executive, Family and Organizational Life* (New York: New American Library, 1980), pp. 32 *ff.*

8. In addition to the Maces' summary of studies, above, see Richard A. Hunt, *Ministry & Marriage* (Dallas: Ministry Studies Board, 1976).

9. For intentional ministry designs see John Biersdorf, ed. *Creating an Intentional Ministry* (Nashville: Abingdon Press, 1976); and Robert D. Dale, *To Dream Again* (Nashville: Broadman Press, 1981).

10. See David Augsburger, *Anger and Assertiveness in Pastoral Care* (Philadelphia: Fortress Press, 1979); and Dan Bagby, *Anger in the Church* (Nashville: Broadman Press, 1979).

11. Greiff and Munter, *Tradeoffs,* pp. 34 *ff.*

10 Transitions:
Trusting God in the Seasons of Life

A striking feature of all that has been said about the life and work of persons on mission for God is the requisite of their resolute faith in Him. In chapter 1, ministers and missionaries were identified as "fools for Christ's sake" (1 Cor. 4:9-10). The image of wise folly was used because their religious orientation often appears impractical, even incongruous, to persons who pursue earthly goals rather than service to God. Loyalty to "lost," though worthy, causes and support of religious endeavors appear to render ministers misfits who are unsuited for life's stubborn realities.

Alastair Campbell holds that a true image of ministry may be rediscovered in the biblical motif of wise folly. He cited Paul's caution to the Corinthian church concerning worldly wisdom: "If anyone among you thinks that he is wise by this world's standards, he should become a fool, in order to be really wise" (1 Cor. 3:18, GNB). In *Rediscovering Pastoral Care,* Campbell characterizes the wise fool as a person of simple (not cunning) thought and life-style, who is loyal to Christ and filled with prophetic wisdom.[1] He has in mind the insightful medieval sage whose disarming naiveté exposed the world's insincerity and self-deception, not the professional court jester who dared to confront the king. Christ himself, though He is the wisdom of the Father, was viewed as foolish by the very critics He came to save (1 Cor. 1:24-25).

Understanding the paradox of wise folly will help laypersons support the religious leader's direct way of relating to other people, appreciate his self-denying commitments, and ponder why God seems to demand so much in a life beset by stress. Furthermore, a lay support community will recognize the ordinariness of persons who offer them Christ on Sunday and provide care during the struggles of every week.

In this chapter we shall see how Christian caregivers are compelled to live courageously by faith. Like you, the reader, they must cope with contradictions and search for some sign that things are all right even when everything seems horribly wrong. We are asking how individual caregivers acquire and maintain a sense of orientation in life's ongoing process of change. Where does one find stability, order, continuity, and a comprehensive perspective mid the fragmented, disruptive, and uprooted experiences of Christian ministry? God's servants cannot manage life as well as they would like, at least not in the secret places. They must endure life's too-muchness as nonheroic, ordinary people who live by faith.

Living as Ordinary People

It appears to be a characteristic of human nature to fantasize that religious leaders live above life's ordinariness. We create illusions of tidy lives for ministers and missionaries. We imagine them safe between Sundays like little plastic soldiers tucked away in preformed, Styrofoam boxes. They never fall down, get dirty, become embarrassed, or mess up things. They are too good, down at the bottom, to get tied into knots with anger or stress. God's invisible hand keeps them out of trouble with a special gift of Christ's grace. Should heartaches come their way, however, we hope they are invincible and will survive.

There is a major problem with such fantasies. They frequently force ordained ministers of the gospel to live a charade. My contention here is that a perfectionistic minister cannot keep his or her little cosmos in complete control. No matter how urgently the world says, "You're *special!*" each Christian caregiver desires to be an ordinary person before God.

Judith Guest's novel *Ordinary People* gave many readers and film viewers a new perspective of the meaning of being human.[2] Becoming ordinary, not different or special, is the symbolic goal for which the main character of her novel searches. He is seventeen-year-old Conrad Jarrett, catapulted into suicidal depression by the accidental drowning of his older brother, Buck. The story reveals complex relationships: Conrad to himself, wondering why he was spared in a boating accident that took Buck's life; to his parents, who have lost control of their lives; to his psychiatrist, Dr. Berger, a savior-figure in the story; to his adolescent world; and of his parents to each other.

Targeted for death, grief, parental conflict, teenage depression and attempted suicide, plus an extended mental hospital stay for Conrad, the Jarretts sought to settle the past and become common people again. Their experience becomes illustrative of misadventures many religious workers might share. The world viewed Calvin and Beth Jarrett as competent, successful, beautiful parents. This family had it *all.* Yet, experienced internally, Conrad wanted to die as punishment for having survived when Buck drowned. A highly controlled mother found herself unable to cope when the foundations of her life shattered following her favorite son's death. The father felt helpless when the two people closest to him were hurting alone, out of his reach.

Conrad's self-appraisal of being different, unheroic, powerless, and trapped in the malaise of "no-win" relationships parallels the lives of some preachers and missionaries' kids. He is confused by life, full of neurotic guilt for being alive when his brighter, "better" brother is dead. Conrad sees himself as "unusual" in comparison with other students at his high school. All he wants is to be rid of the past and become an ordinary teenager again. This was the desire of his parents for their lives, too. If only things were like they were *before!*

Earlier, in chapter 4, we observed that religious workers long anxiously for a place—a home for the heart—in a world where they don't quite fit. As youth they were advised to grow up and "fit into" an adult world. In the young adult era, after responding to God's call for ministry or missions, they faced the necessity of letting go their settled places, families, and jobs. Meantime, their security lies within God's call as they search for reliable orientation mid continuous change.

We understand the external transitions folks face in young, middle, and late adulthood as children grow up, and parents age and die. It is the internal changes—so real and troublesome to the human spirit, and visible primarily to God—that laypersons miss. When a person or couple gives life to God in Christian service, there is a relative loss of control. Self-control is surrendered to divine authority and to the care of members of congregations, mission sponsors, or nationals overseas.

It is the basic theme of self-control, its loss through life's chances, and Conrad Jarrett's efforts to regain order in his life that makes *Ordinary People* so compelling for us. By choice, chance, and circumstance, ministers give up control of their lives. Their salvation lies not only in the practice of trusting God but in the grip He holds on their lives. Ultimately, as Jesus expressed it, their security lies in the assurance that "no one can snatch them away from the Father's care" (John 10:28-29, GNB).

Christian caregivers place their lives in the hands of a higher Power. Such is the essence of faith. In Guest's plot, both Conrad and his father place their lives in the hands of a care figure—psychiatrist Berger. Conrad grew to appreciate the counseling sessions, for they brought clarification and stability to his life. The "shrink" became his friend and expressed hope that Conrad would "let the man out of the closet." What a discovery! His physician wanted him to become a real person and assume responsibility for his life.

Becoming *ordinary* for Conrad involved experiencing life in both its goodness and badness. He started therapy with Dr. Berger, denying his feelings while, at the same time, conveying anger and grief. One day he experienced profound pain, and Berger explained that feelings are not selective. When "you can't feel pain, you aren't gonna feel anything else, either. And the world is full of pain. Also joy. Evil. Goodness. Horror and love. You name it, it's there. Sealing yourself off is just going through the motions, get it?"[3] With this wisdom Conrad received the key of the door to being a normal, ordinary person. The teenager had not faced up to the pain/joy of life. He had been unwilling or unable to see life's bittersweet for all it's meant to be.

The novel ends paradoxically with the Jarretts breaking up, at least temporarily. Beth leaves Calvin and returns to her brother's home in Houston. Thus, Conrad and his father pass each other on the road which average people travel. As the book ends, he asks his father, "How did everything fall apart like this?" To which the elder Jarrett replied, "It's nobody's fault. . . . It is the way things are." Ordinariness, then, does not imply the absence of self-doubt, pain, and sorrow; rather, the acceptance of the shadow side of good. Given that insight, the book's nonhero was placed in touch with hope, no matter what lay ahead.

Ministers and missionaries, akin to the Jarretts in at least one respect, are acquainted with loss, separation, and grief. They are continually weaned from one set of attachments and attracted to others on the journey of faith. Missionaries, for example, leave parents and eventually children, homeland, established roles, accomplishments, possessions, and support groups in America for an unstable, overseas world. Investing heavily in prayer, spiritual seeking, Bible study, and submission to God's will, old attachments lose their power. This is not to say that former activities and relationships totally disappear. They just become less important and less demanding of time and energy.

Profound spiritual pursuit and weaning from earlier attachments "represents a loss," notes psychiatrist Gerald May, "not a loss of things themselves, but of one's investment in them. Even so, it is a very real loss, and at some level, what is lost will be mourned."[4] Laypersons who would truly help ministers need to understand that heartaches will happen regardless of the aura around God's servants or of new freedoms discovered in their leaving old attachments. In some respects, the loss of former attachments intensifies feelings of nonbelonging that surface wherever a minister or missionary serves. Home is harder to keep up with. New relationships keep forming, perhaps stronger than the old ones. With frequent moves, there may be only a limited time to mourn the loss of former ties before investing in new, deeper attachments.

We have been reminded that God's servants struggle somehow for normalcy despite feelings of unordinariness. Looking at one minister's experiences can help us to understand the trauma of temporariness and value of faith in the seasons of life.

One Minister's Passages

Ralph Loe married shortly after his return to a Christian college campus following World War II. He was of conservative religious persuasion and was viewed as quite intelligent by his bride, Melinda Jackson Loe, and other persons who knew him.

Their early years were marked by limited finances and budget restrictions, plus inadequate time together since both of them were still in school. Also, Ralph served a student pastorate. Pressures mounted: from parental expectations for them to get established financially, from personal desires to achieve in school, and from physical exhaustion because of the church assignment on weekends.

Entering the adult world involves expectations from both sets of parents that a young couple succeed vocationally, *not* bear children prematurely ("before thay can afford one"), yet *not* wait so long for kids that grandparenting is out of the question. Melinda wanted a child long before Ralph was prepared for the challenges, risks, and responsibilities of parenting. A daughter was born during their "push/pull" seminary years, while they were still in their mid-twenties. About the same time, Melinda's businessman father died from a heart attack. A major pillar in their support system was gone.

Being a pastor of persons in a rural Southern setting compounded Ralph's anxiety about economic, educational, and vocational issues. He discovered that a big decision in a small church could impose a loss of direction in his family's life. Major differences of opinion among members, plus criticism, were occasions of anguish. Other people's expectations were superimposed upon his own. As a seminary pastor his words didn't amount to much with either his theological faculty or his congregants. Living on the ragged edges of energy, time, and money, Ralph worked hard at being husband, father, student, pastor, son to his parents, and denominational loyalist. Aspirations waned as expectations mounted. Depression became a constant companion. Ralph hoped a rebirth would occur by moving his little family two thousand miles to a different academic setting. He tried to convince Melinda that God was in it.

While the Loes were still in early adulthood, their obligations increased. The family moved so that the young husband/father could pursue advanced studies at a theological school in the North. They lived on a "shoestring," so Melinda sought employment. Ralph, meanwhile, worked in a mission church situation and pursued graduate studies in theology. A second child was born, a son. Meanwhile, the young father became disillusioned with his doctoral program. Some family conflicts grew out of Ralph's and Melinda's maturational problems and situational concerns.

As Ralph entered what Daniel Levinson called the "age 30

transition," he moved his family again. Disappointed with certain administrative shifts and policy decisions in his professional studies, he entered a third institution of higher learning for doctoral degree work. He persuaded Melinda it was God's will. Presbyterian writer John Killinger describes the impatience and exuberance of youthful clergy as "learning to wait for the kingdom" of God.[5] He compares youth's impatience with the System to the disciples' offer to call down fire from heaven upon reluctant recruits in Jesus' day (Luke 9:51-56). Rather than wishing to remake the world, as Killinger holds concerning youthful ministers, Ralph's family sought survival and certitude.

My own research with young ministers does not match precisely Killinger's assumption that beginning clergy push impetuously to change the System. Rather, they wonder who has sufficient wisdom and power to change radically the way things are. Agreed, youth bring energy, ambition, and unbridled enthusiasm, drive, and devotion to life's assignments. Yet, viewed in retrospect, the earliest stage of ministry is perceived by most clergy as a low point of life because of their lack of experience, wisdom, education, political savvy, and self-confidence. To his credit, Killinger prefaced his sermonic essays with support for the contributions young preachers have made to the church. In reality, however, the System appears too complex, awesome, and unmalleable to yield easily to youth's decisive pressure.

As Ralph and Melinda Loe transitioned into early mid-life, they decided together to seek mission appointment from a major board. Their postdoctoral assignment was with a church in a county-seat town. While it was a good match and they "loved the people," traditional pastoral work eventually became routine. The challenging edges wore off. An earlier vision of world missions, involving theological education of national pastors, carried them into new experiences—language school, acculturation, settling in, bonding with other missionaries and national leaders, and learning to trust God for family care.

One term of mission service followed by a furlough from the field found the Loes parents for the third time—another daughter. Tasks widened in additional terms of service. As the years passed, mission demands increased. The children grew up and went overseas to college in the United States, at least two of them did. Their youngest child tried it away from home awhile, then returned to a national educational center. She met and married a seminarian in their instructional setting. Now, they have several children and major professional responsibilities outside the United States.

Ralph and Melinda Loe eventually became senior members of their Mission. Their influence with local leaders had increased across the years. He was a respected preacher, teacher, and institutional administrator. They had endured upheavals of several moves and had lived in a number of different settings during twenty-five years of service. With family grown and gone, the Loes faced the possibility of decreased space for housing provision. Their aging parents claimed more attention and investment of concern. In time, both of Ralph's parents died and Melinda's widowed mother became restricted in activity. In his late fifties, Ralph sought a new assignment—a change of careers within the Mission. He opted out of a confining administrative post and into an exciting pastoral assignment. This transition, in turn, changed his relationships and responsibilities with the national convention by reducing his role, status, and authority. It seemed a wise move for culminating his missions career.

Self-care made Ralph aware of the value of spiritual disciplines. He grew increasingly monastic and maintained a rigorous spiritual devotion before God. Health care pushed him to an active, regular exercise program. He was exacting in matters pertaining to both spiritual and physical health. Domestic and grandparenting tasks occupied Melinda's time and energies.

Today, retirement looms ahead. The need for a place in the USA to call *home* faces them. The Loes enjoy their extended family. They are proud of their children, grandchildren, and promise of another generation. Retirement options are being explored. Unfinished tasks lie ahead. Nationals are being encouraged to transfer loyalties to younger, newer missionaries. The future beckons with plans to place mission matters in younger persons' hands, retire with Social Security and Board benefits, and return to America for ministries that health and opportunities permit. Such are the seasons of one minister's life.

Ordinary People provided a mirror to observe potential flash points for growth or regression for God's servants. It helped us to sense that Christian professionals are more human than otherwise. Next, we observed one family's process of interpreting God's leadership through major developmental eras and obeying His dynamic call. We sensed how urgent it becomes to feel God's grip on our lives, not merely to hang on by trusting Him. Now we ask what ministry faith provides in life's transitions.

The Ministry Faith Provides

The Bible says no one can please God without faith (Heb. 11:6). Why must Christian servants be *true believers,* not faithless, but believable messengers sent from God? Is it not because of the services healthy faith renders in the seasons of life? Beyond saving faith itself, like that Jesus pictured in John 3 and elsewhere, what tasks does faith perform?

One, biblical faith provides a basic orientation to human existence. One understands oneself in the midst of all spatial and temporal changes because life's compass hand is fixed on true North— the reality of God. Laypersons are obligated to help caregivers find and maintain a "fix" on the Father's redemptive purpose for mankind. Christians are pilgrim people who desperately desire reliable patterns for their lives. Faith provides *reference points* for locating oneself in the journey through life. One soon learns whether or not one is on or off course in the trajectory of life's purpose. Faith inspires a sense of *continuity* with believers in all periods of biblical and human history. One does not have to "reinvent the wheel" of Christian story and mission. Rather, each generation celebrates religious experience, interprets it theologically in historic context, then shares it with other believers.

Faith calls to mind meaningful *ritual processes* like altar building and sacrifices of a "contrite heart" from the Old Testament, worship and symbols like baptism and the Lord's Supper from the New Testament. In the prophetic tradition, faithful persons seek justice for their fellow travelers on planet earth. While love may appear an "impossible possibility" in international affairs and labor/management relations, for example, justice seeks what is fair and right under the law. In the wisdom tradition of Job, Proverbs, and Ecclesiastes one observes the management of severe suffering, resolution of moral confusion in relationships, and effort to comprehend life's meaning and purpose. Much of Jesus' teaching and practice of religion was founded in these Old Testament patterns. His convincing sense of mission sustained him in hostile environments. Jesus' model of faith inspires our own quiet resolve and instills serenity in the face of alien or hostile forces.

Two, faith inspires coherent development within the unfolding seasons of life. Linked to our understandings of human growth and aging, faith enables appropriate responses to life's developmental crises. Writers like Erik Erikson remind us that healthy persons experience growth in recognizable stages. His "Eight Stages of Man," first presented in *Childhood and Society,* propose age-appropriate tasks, polarities of achievement and failure, and virtues corresponding to each stage.[6] Our concern here is not with the details of Eriksonian theory except as they apply to adults. He pictured the central task of adulthood as *generativity*—caring for members of the coming generation—and demonstrated how that stage depends upon successful accomplishments in preadult years.

An important feature of Erikson's life-cycle theory is the thesis that each stage is bipolar—*this* vs. *that*—with one positive and one negative pole. The opposite of generativity for adults, for example, is *stagnation*. This implies that one may become so fully absorbed in his or her own welfare, status, or problems that no energy remains for one's own children. The key virture of the generative adult is *care,* according to Erikson's moral foundation for his stages published in *Insight and Responsibility.*[7] While his observations of human growth were made quite apart from biblical revelation, Erikson appreciates religious traditions and cites Scriptures in his writings. Additionally, he has authored major psychological biographies of Martin Luther and Mohandas Gandhi, with appreciation for religious patterns in their development.

Three, faith moves God's person toward health and wholeness in the adult individuation process. "But how?" you ask. Four tasks of middle adulthood appeared in the research of psychologist Daniel J. Levinson, of Yale Medical School. He led a team of researchers in studying the personalities of forty men, in four career groups, for ten years. The subjects were in mid-life, between the ages of thirty-five and forty-five. His *The Seasons of a Man's Life* revealed four opposing growth directions to manage in middle adulthood: young/old attitudes, destructive/creative acts of behavior, masculine/feminine tendencies, and attached/separate relational patterns. Managing such polarities, originating in oneself and society, is a major assignment in the middle years.

The Levinson research group used the term *polarity* "in the sense that the two terms represent opposing tendencies or conditions."[8] It would appear superficially that a person grows in one direction or the other but not both. In actuality, Levinson noted, "the paired tendencies are not mutually exclusive. Both sides of each polarity coexist within every self."[9] Polar tensions are experienced by all persons, leading to productive or destructive life-styles. How does personal faith help someone discipline these internal, often unconscious, processes? We respond by examining three opposing tendencies of middle adulthood.

In middle age, one is no longer physically young; yet, neither does one wish to appear old. Why is this so? *Youth,* noted Levinson, symbolizes growth, openness, energy, and potential as well as impulsiveness, inexperience, and fragility. Young persons appear to possess a future full of promise. They symbolize vitality and a vision of things to come. Conversely, *old* in Western culture represents winding down, completion of life, then death. Active individuals in mid-life shrink from the impotence and disconnectedness of later adulthood. They count the energies, potentials, and options of the young. A major assignment of one in middle life "is to confront the Young and the Old within oneself and seek new ways of being Young/Old."[10] The pulls of Young and Old poles are experienced throughout the human life cycle, are modified, and placed in new balance. Faith accepts the tensions within us as shaping forces, modified by experience, over the course of one's life.

The Destruction/Creation polarity represents the death/life impulses within each of us. In middle age one becomes more aware of one's mortality and of the possible death of others around him. Life has been hurtful in many ways; other persons may have acted destructively toward him. They may have neglected, opposed, or actually wished him dead. On the other hand, an individual realizes he has hurt those he claims to love—parents, spouse, children, siblings, friends, competitors—along the way. Now, he craves a more creative epoch of peaceful relationships with old enemies. There is longing to participate in causes that advance human welfare and guarantee good gifts for generations that follow. One resolves to move beyond conflict to reintegration of destructive and creative forces which coexist in the human spirit.

We shall illustrate one further polarity which faith in God helps us master: attachment/separateness. The researchers viewed attachment broadly to encompass all forces that connect a person with his environment. To be attached, they said, is to feel plugged in, engaged, involved, or participating with persons and events; separateness denotes involvement in one's own inner world of imagination, fantasy, or play. "His main interest is not in adapting to the 'real' world outside, but in constructing and exploring an imagined world, the enclosed world of his inner self."[11] Thus, separateness must be distinguised from isolation or aloneness. One can be alone, planning some activity or feeling resentment over past rejection, and still be engaged with the world.

Elaborating on these inner pulls persons feel, life underscores the need for direction—human and divine. Faith seeks a way to integrate each polarity and energize creative future development. To the extent one fails, one forms inner contradictions that will cloud the next transition. Levinson holds that it is human both to fail and succeed in these integrative assignments at every age. Faith seeks a way to succeed in such private struggles, yet assures divine forgiveness when one has failed.

Interestingly, the orientation faith provides changes since faith itself undergoes stages along life's way. The research of James Fowler and associates at Harvard University, with hundreds of individuals from childhood to old age, disclosed that healthy faith changes with age and wisdom.[12] It matures from the mythic/literal grasp of a child's reality to the universal perception of a Mohandas Gandhi, Martin Luther King, Jr., or Mother Teresa.

Thus far we have seen that faith provides God's persons with reliable patterns, reference points, and ritual processes for life. Trusting Providence supports a coherent existence and inspires health and wholeness through the aging process.

There is yet another ministry faith provides. *Four, trusting God's redemptive activity in history helps his servants set appropriate limits for their vocations.* Within the body of Christ, each man or woman is free to explore gifts and graces and to practice his or her calling. Fidelity to God's saving purpose lends authenticity to one's practice of ministry. One leads, evangelizes, encourages, teaches, or interprets with accountability both to God and one's people in particular contexts (1 Cor. 12—14). One person cannot do everything in ministry or missions, but one can do his or her calling for God.

Since ministers and missionaries recognize their limits as ordinary people in extraordinary callings, are there models in the Bible of authentic faith in God? Yes. Laypersons wishing to help their professional caregivers can point them toward committed predecessors on the journey of faith.

Biblical Models of Faith

The eleventh chapter of Hebrews provides a roll call of exemplers of the faith during Old Testament eras. Models of spiritual sensitivity, holy boldness, intuitive trust, steadfastness in suffering, inspiring leadership, and obedient service picture historic results of fidelity to God. Jewish Christian readers could identify with innovators of hope in ancient Israel who proclaimed justice, exposed sin, faced opposition, built cities, and endured hardships because they were people of faith. Any person who longs for something better in life and shrinks from spiritual or psychological depletion is a candidate for such commitment. That is certainly true of men and women in ministry today.

Ancients in the biblical story gained orientation in an unstable world through personal faith and corporate loyalty to God. In Abraham, the Jews became God's chosen people. When the, national sense of a favored destiny eroded and the land deteriorated under disobedient rulers, faith was reborn through God's fidelity to His promises. Prophetic deliverers appeared at

times of overwhelming need with encouragement from the
Lord. Hope held that someday a Redeemer would come—the
promised Messiah—to bless the world through Israel. Persons
who dared to arrogate power to themselves, apart from God,
were punished. Unfaithful individuals became the losers in the
long pull of history. Restoration of personal confidence and
national purpose came as individual faith was renewed.

In picturing Christ as mediator of a new covenant, the writer
of Hebrews reminded his readers of God's trustworthiness.
"Hence we can confidently say," he quoted an ancient psalmist, " 'The Lord is my helper, I will not be afraid; what can man
do to me?' " (Heb. 13:6; Ps. 118:6). They were to remember
their leaders—"those who spoke to you the word of God"—
consider the outcome of their experience and "imitate their
faith" (Heb. 13:7). That is God's eternal invitation to His servants in all eras of history.

What was true in biblical story remains valid in human
experience. When gloom settles over the life of a man, woman,
family, or nation, faith cuts through to God's promised deliver-
ance. We are still inspired by Christian heroes and heroines
who serve in missions and ministry around the world. Damp-
ening that faith, squelching that hope, smothering that love is
a sin from which laypersons shrink. Our need is to affirm,
challenge, pray for, and encourage God's servants wherever
they may minister.

Like you, the reader, Christian pastors, denominational executives, teachers, missionaries, chaplains, and others in ministry vocations must trust God in the seasons of life. Such hope
cannot be ordered into being. It does not ride on the wings of
good advice or surge from the depths of cutting criticism. Faith
and hope, like love, are relational virtues, not abstractions. The
capacity to trust God in all seasons is one of life's most significant potentials. The true believer possesses a sense of destiny,
direction, and divinely ordered energy to inspire other persons.
In order to help your minister, be counted for Christ and his

cause wherever you live on earth. So shall you share his call, his cross, his final commendation.

To summarize, we have pictured the lives of God's servants as ordinary people. Human events and expectations often thrust them into conflicting, almost impossible, circumstances. Being sensitive to God's will, they appear impractical, even foolish at times, to hardheaded realists. The minister's passages through life seem helter-skelter, lacking a single thread of purpose and internal consistency. They often appear to be running away from some intractable wilderness or insidious enemy rather than running toward God.

"Such a waste," we muse of mobile ministers and humble missionaries whose lives bloom like roses in desert places. No, they are not crusaders for earth's lost causes. They are champions of righteousness, not their own but of the King of kings and Lord of lords. They love you, so *love them back* faithfully and well.

Notes

1. Alastair V. Campbell, *Rediscovering Pastoral Care* (Philadelphia: Westminster Press, 1981), pp. 55-65.

2. Judith Guest, *Ordinary People* (New York: Viking Press, 1976); (New York: Ballentine Press, 1980); (Penguin paperback, 1982), a secular novel with profoundly human implications.

3. Ibid., Ballentine ed., p. 209.

4. Gerald G. May, M.D., *Care of Mind Care of Spirit: Psychiatric Dimensions of Spiritual Direction* (San Francisco: Harper & Row, 1982), p. 81.

5. John Killinger, *Christ in the Seasons of Ministry* (Waco: Word Books, 1981), pp. 19-38.

6. Erik H. Erikson, *Childhood and Society*, 2d rev. ed. (New York: W. W. Norton, Co., 1963), chapter 7.

7. Erik H. Erikson, *Insight and Responsibility* (New York: W. W. Norton, Co., 1964).

8. Daniel J. Levinson, *The Seasons of a Man's Life* (New York: Alfred A. Knopf, 1978), p. 197.

9. Ibid.

10. Ibid., p. 210.

11. Ibid., p. 239.

12. James W. Fowler, *The Stages of Faith* (San Francisco: Harper & Row, 1981).

Appendixes

Alternatives to Forced Termination
by
James L. Cooper, Coordinator
Ministers Counseling Service
Baptist General Convention of Texas

Since so much is being written about it these days, it would appear that forced termination is in epidemic proportions. I think this is not the case, though there are certainly far more forced terminations than are necessary. I contend that there are some viable alternatives which, if pursued, would eliminate many involuntary resignations.

The first suggestion would be for the pastor to select a representative group with whom to meet at least twice a year to discuss the progress of the church, especially as it relates to his ministry. This group should not be all "yes men." Such feedback could ward off much potential conflict.

Second, churches might look with favor on providing a program of continuing education for their minister, either on a yearly basis or a sabbatical. These would be designed for the minister's own spiritual renewal and/or sharpening his skills in areas of deficiency. I am thinking of such opportunities as the Personal and Professional Growth Course, involving two weeks, provided by the Career Guidance Section of the Baptist Sunday School Board or the mini terms (approximately four weeks) offered by a number of seminaries. If the study leave came at five-year intervals, then as much as three or four months might be considered.

Third, churches could encourage ministers to consider the many opportunities for counseling and/or career assessment which are available through many sources.

Fourth, try letting the leader lead. Any organization including the church needs a leader, a chief administrative officer. I understand the pastor to hold that position in the New Testament perspective—not as an autocratic dictator—but as a spiritual overseer. Admittedly, the pastor does not possess a straight line to God, but neither do a few members have that kind of monopoly. In many experiences of church conflict there exists a struggle for leadership between the pastor and some power structure within the congregation, usually consisting of from one to a dozen or more. For the sake of the church, the congregation may need to encourage a more constructive working relationship between these two entities.

Fifth, a conflict mediator might be a wise investment. So many times, in heated conflict, neither congregation nor minister can be objective; thus, an outsider could help to clarify the issues and determine redemptive alternatives. As a result, a person's ministry and a church's reputation may be salvaged.

Sixth, if no satisfactory solution can be found or accepted, then the minister should be given adequate time to relocate while remaining in his present

215

staff position. It is difficult enough for a minister to relocate while under pressure, but it is even more difficult if he has already been terminated. It is easier to move somewhere from someplace than to move somewhere from nowhere. This grace period will save face for both minister and congregation.

There may be times, when every alternative has been exhausted, that forced termination is the only avenue left. In that event, let the record always show that the church—the body of Christ—has acted with grace and generosity. In the simplest form this would involve providing adequate severance pay up to a minimum of six months, or until the minister is gainfully employed. Thirty days is simply not enough provision, and anything less is either coldhearted or punitive!

There are valid reasons for continuing the minister's salary, housing, and hospitalization insurance for at least six months. First, unlike a person in other professions, a minister cannot walk up to a pastorless church and present his application. This practice, though acceptable in the business world, is unacceptable in the religious realm. Consider also the fact that the normal process of moving from one church to another, even under favorable conditions, takes a number of months.

Second, a minister's theological education is not a marketable commodity in the secular world. It therefore takes more time to find church-related employment.

Third, the specter of financial bankruptcy faces the minister. Unless he or she is employed soon, he stands to lose his life insurance, his automobile and house (if these are still mortgaged), and exhaust his life's savings. In this day of exorbitant medical costs, a person or family cannot afford to be without hospitalization insurance.

Fourth, the church paid his moving expenses to the city where he has served, but who will pay his moving expenses now that he may have to relocate? If his salary is continued, he will be in a better position to handle this himself.

Fifth, even if the pastor has been terminated for justifiable grounds, his wife and children are seldom to blame. The innocent should not be called on to suffer along with the guilty.

I plead for churches to "go the second mile" in providing financial assistance to the terminated minister and his family. I believe that Christ would approve.

Model Pastor-Church Covenant
Hatcher Memorial Baptist Church, Richmond, Virginia

Cover Letter

DEAR MEMBERS OF HATCHER,

The relationship between a church and its pastor is not an employer-employee one. It is basically a covenant, not a contract, because the element of trust is involved. A covenant is not a legal document but some promises that Christian people make to each other in the church. This is also a good definition of a covenant for the pastor-church relationship.

The idea of a covenant is not new to most Baptist churches since most use the same one. A written covenant between the pastor and the church is a logical outgrowth of the church covenant concept. Verbal agreements are easily forgotten. The church-pastor covenant, with God as the "third partner," begins a relationship subject to the crisis, periods of adjustment, and psychological process typical of a human relationship. The process is often marked by struggles over who is going to be in charge, who will have "the last word," etc. A written covenant will help to avoid such misunderstandings and problems.

The ideal time for a pastor and church to enter into a covenant relationship is when a new pastor is coming to a church. The prospective pastor and search committee can discuss things together before the relationship is finalized. Churches and pastors often have unrealistic expectations of each other and misunderstand their obligations to each other.

Not only the search committee, the deacons, and the finance committee need to understand the terms of the covenant agreement, but the whole church membership also. A covenant that is printed and distributed will help eliminate misunderstandings about the financial and time arrangements, as well as provisions for the pastor's housing and utilities.

The covenant can also be used for reviewing the status of the relationship. Churches and pastors need to understand and talk about the sometimes hidden meaning of what is happening between them. This should be a mutual thing with each feeling free to talk about how both are measuring up to expectations and obligations. Obviously there should be provisions made for making changes in the covenant relationship, especially for financial and time arrangements.

There is ample room in a healthy relationship for a diversity of opinions. The problem in many churches is that we do not "speak the truth to one another in love" (as Paul recommends), but we tend to talk "about" one another instead of "with" one another. Churches and pastor are often embarrassed by conflict and will not open themselves to counseling by objective outsiders. Many very difficult situations can be averted if help is accepted early enough.

217

When a pastor and a church "most solemnly and joyfully enter into a covenant with one another," the outcome will be a better relationship and understanding as they seek to do the Lord's work together.

LOVE IN CHRIST,

YOUR PASTOR SEARCH COMMITTEE

Covenant for Pastor-Church Relationship

The Pastor's Expectations of His Church
1. Trust in him as a person of integrity dedicated to the work of the ministry and as a competent professional person who can manage the use of his time wisely.
2. Support for him as a leader by faithful stewardship in coming, giving, and serving in the church along with recognition when his work is well done.
3. Consultation with him about church affairs before decisions are made so that the church can benefit from his training and experience and so that the work of the church can be coordinated.
4. Authority for him to approve or disapprove the coming of other ministers and religious groups to the church and to supervise all paid employees of the church.

The Church's Expectations of Its Pastor
1. Competency in ministry through well-prepared sermons, regular visitation where there is a need, pastoral care in crisis situations, administrative and organizational leadership, and the improvement of pastoral skills through continued study.
2. Availability by having it announced when and where he can be contacted during the week and by letting it be known how he can be contacted while he is away from the church field.
3. Leadership in worship services, evangelistic outreach efforts, the development of a Christian education program, and the administrative work of the church in cooperation with the church's leaders.
4. Loyalty to Baptist beliefs as found in the Scriptures, attendance at denominational meetings, and support for the Cooperative Program.
5. Participation in civic and community affairs and cooperation with compatable interdenominational endeavors in the area.

The Pastor's Obligation to His Church
1. To fulfill the duties of the office of pastor as a servant of the church rather than the church's ruler who always knows what is best.
2. To seek to meet the spiritual needs of his people through biblical preaching and teaching and to refrain from proclaiming his own opinions as the Word of God.
3. To meet the reasonable expectations of the congregation for him as its minister while at the same time living his own life as he believes God would have him to do.
4. To manage his money with integrity so as not to bring reproach upon the church.
5. To accept the church as an imperfect organization composed of imperfect people who must be loved and forgiven, to work with the elected leaders of the church, and to try to be the pastor of all the people in the church.
6. To acknowledge that constructive criticism from the congregation can be helpful and to be open enough to accept it and profit by it.
7. To recognize the need for help from outside the church when his role as pastor is endangered and to avoid actions that would harm the church.
8. To serve within the guidelines of our church constitution and bylaws.

The Church's Obligation to Its Pastor
1. To respect the office of pastor and to support his ministry for as long as he holds that office to which the church has called him.
2. To guarantee the freedom of the pulpit, so the pastor can preach his convictions in his own manner and style as the Spirit of God leads him.
3. To allow the pastor to be himself instead of trying to fit him into some ministerial mold and to expect no more of his family than any other family in the church.
4. To provide the pastor's support to the best of the church's ability and to review annually the pastor's compensation as an evidence of the church's care and concern for his welfare.
5. To recognize that because the pastor is human he makes mistakes and needs forgiveness like everyone else and that because of the limitation of time he cannot do all that he should do and fulfill everybody's expectations.
6. To confer with the pastor about any accusation made against him instead of discussing it in secret and to refrain from passing judgment upon him until he has had the opportunity to defend himself.
7. To counsel with the pastor when there is a disruptive conflict involving him and to give him adequate time to relocate if he needs to move.

Matters of Mutual Agreement
1. When the pastor moves to the community in which the church is located, the church shall pay his moving expenses.
2. If there is a disruptive conflict in the church, the pastor and the deacons shall mutually agree to seek competent help from outside the church membership to meet with them and advise them about solving their problems.

Denominational Support for Ministers/Missionaries

The author sent questionnaires to chief executives of thirty representative Protestant denominations in the USA in an attempt to assess what the denominations are now doing. He asked what kinds of action were being taken currently to address the issue of caring for pastors, church staff members, and missionaries.

Replies came from twenty-three officials—a 77 percent return—which was excellent. The following items represent the efforts of denominations which replied.

Likely, the denominations that responded were those which have taken some action or have considered clergy support programs. Several executives sent copies of formal program statements. Other groups are in process of considering care ministries for professional caregivers. All respondents acknowledged that their particular group had investigated clergy/missionary support needs. Such evidence suggests that at least some major denominational groups are aware of, and concerned about, the need for caring for their own professional caregivers. Such efforts should be intensified in the future.

Statements About Ministry—Our Denomination	Yes	No	No Response
Has investigated clergy/missionary support needs	23		
Has appointed a person to explore clergy care issues	14	6	3
Limits concern for ministers to retirement annuities	2	20	1
Has held a consultation on caring for ministers	19	2	2
Provides family enrichment programs for clergy	15	6	2
Provides career guidance/mid-career evaluation	12	9	2
Provides placement (church/minister) services	21	1	1
Published a report of some kind (please attach)	8	10	5
Support system confined to local congregation	3	19	1
Has developed a national counseling referral network	11	10	2

How Christians in the USA Can Help Missionaries
Both on the Field and During Furlough

1. Provide furnished missionary housing, with adequate storage space, while on furlough. Consider them your missionary family-in-residence.
2. Provide an insured, dependable car for furloughing missionaries—*not* for sale. Give it to them to use and return at the end of furlough.
3. Be well informed. What people are *up* on they're not *down* on. *Really* knowing what missionaries are doing makes them feel cared for.
4. Stay in touch. We want to hear from you, especially on special days (birthdays, anniversaries). Also, we would like to hear your voices on cassette.
5. Share magazines like *Christianity Today* and *Ladies Home Journal*, and send good books you have enjoyed.
6. Be sensitive and supportive about a missionary's family life. Just as it is difficult to adjust to the field—so it is hard, at times, to readjust to life in the States.
7. Involve missionary kids (MKs) in ministry of local churches. Include MKs in your family circle of sharing and caring.
8. Care for MKs in college away from the family and home. "Adopt" them into your family for Sunday meals, weekend outings, etc. Help MKs with transportation. Remember them at times of special holidays like Christmas, Easter, and Thanksgiving. (I'm an MK, and I'm speaking from warm and fond memories of a loving family that "adopted" me.)
9. Discover how God would have you to be on mission. It is not just "missionaries" who are on mission for God. We support each other greatly in this manner.
10. Book missionary speakers at your church in advance. If a missionary is desired for a service, plan months ahead. Please do not assume they are available the day called or the day after. The day a missionary is in town may be for a medical exam, private family time, or preparation time.
11. Remember missionaries are people like you. They need friends while on furlough as do their children.
12. Accept missionaries' newsletters as letters. Writing time on the field is precious.
13. Encourage missionary family time as a family—not as people always "on display" in a church.
14. Permit missionaries to be human. Be a friend. They are people—with aches, cares, loves, feelings, too.
15. Remember our parents (cards, phone calls, etc.) on their birthdays since we cannot call them ourselves. Support them during sickness, surgery, and other crises.

16. I would appreciate used Sunday School and/or VBS materials for use with my children.
17. Care about volunteers' children and grandchildren left behind who may not have other family nearby.
18. Church and state convention papers help keep missionaries informed and morale high. If the church and state convention papers could be airmailed, we could keep up to date with Baptist events.
19. We often need GA materials. It would be helpful if our churches airmailed these materials or sent them with persons traveling to our country.
20. Mail newsletters for missionaries in the USA. Someone in Burundi said: "It costs us about $1.00 to mail one air letter to the US. Helping with duplicating and mailing a periodic newsletter is a great help to us."